with lc

Robert Contrall

THE FALL OF
MY LIFE

The Fall of My Life

Robert Cantrall

BALBOA
PRESS
A DIVISION OF HAY HOUSE

Copyright © 2013 Robert Cantrall.

All rights reserved. No part of this book may be used or reproduced by any means, graphic, electronic, or mechanical, including photocopying, recording, taping or by any information storage retrieval system without the written permission of the publisher except in the case of brief quotations embodied in critical articles and reviews.

Balboa Press books may be ordered through booksellers or by contacting:

Balboa Press
A Division of Hay House
1663 Liberty Drive
Bloomington, IN 47403
www.balboapress.com
1-(877) 407-4847

Because of the dynamic nature of the Internet, any web addresses or links contained in this book may have changed since publication and may no longer be valid. The views expressed in this work are solely those of the author and do not necessarily reflect the views of the publisher, and the publisher hereby disclaims any responsibility for them.

The author of this book does not dispense medical advice or prescribe the use of any technique as a form of treatment for physical, emotional, or medical problems without the advice of a physician, either directly or indirectly. The intent of the author is only to offer information of a general nature to help you in your quest for emotional and spiritual well-being. In the event you use any of the information in this book for yourself, which is your constitutional right, the author and the publisher assume no responsibility for your actions.

Any people depicted in stock imagery provided by Thinkstock are models, and such images are being used for illustrative purposes only. Certain stock imagery © Thinkstock.

Printed in the United States of America.

ISBN: 978-1-4525-7680-0 (sc)
ISBN: 978-1-4525-7681-7 (hc)
ISBN: 978-1-4525-7682-4 (e)

Library of Congress Control Number: 2013911106

Balboa Press rev. date: 07/02/2013

Contents

Thank You ix
Acknowledgments xi
Preface xiii

Chapter 1—Resources 1
Chapter 2—Fear 25
Chapter 3—Anxiety and Depression 59
Chapter 4—Reality 91
Chapter 5—Mechanics 117
Chapter 6—Relationships 137
Chapter 7—The Rest of the Story 159
Chapter 8—The Next Chapter 173

Epilogue 195
Appendix 199

Thank You

To John and Carla Kelly at the Moclips Gull Wing Inn for the perfect setting to write my book. Something very powerful happened in your cottage on the beach that I will never be able to explain.

Acknowledgments

There are so many people I would like to acknowledge for participating in my journey. I am choosing not to list you all here for two reasons. The first is so that I do not leave anyone out, which would be so easy to do because there are so many of you who have blessed my life. The second is that by not producing a list of names, yours is somehow not diminished, for that would be a travesty. I would rather that if somehow you do not think you are one of these people, I should pray for you to know that you are.

Preface

It was the summer of 2008. I was pulling down a comfortable six-figure income and living in a $1.2 million home with waterfront property on Lake Tapps at the foot of Mount Rainier. My wife's was driving her new Lexus, as I drove my red, two-seater Spider convertible. Add in the thirty-six-foot yacht moored in Commencement Bay and christened *Perseverance* and the vacations that allowed us to travel around the states—I was living the American dream. But my life was a big train wreck looking for a place to happen.

The ensuing eight months delivered me unemployment, divorce, foreclosure, repossession, bankruptcy, the death of my brother, and a new life partner. Everyone was impacted by 2008, some internally, some externally, and for the fortunate, both. I was one of the fortunate ones. When I lost my job, as so many others did, I thought I was simply headed out to find a new job once again. Little did I know that I was embarking on a life-changing journey of self-reflection and personal growth.

The pages that follow are an account of my personal journey through the last five years. I did not write this book because I am a doctor, scholar, philosopher, intellectual, teacher or therapist. I share this book only as my personal experience of the events that unfolded over the last five years. Neither do I present any new ideas in this book—any ideas I share are merely my personal application of those I have picked up along the way from people who make a living from creating new ideas, and I am eternally grateful for those people.

It is not of my own doing that these pages came together to form a book, but rather by the undying support of so many others who continually encouraged me until I ultimately felt an undeniable insistence from the universe to share my story. I would like for you to have what I have gained, and I hope to live my life in such a way that you will want what I have found, but without having to experience the depth and breadth of the challenges that I have experienced along the way. I have learned that without these challenges, I would have never gained what I found. I can only hope that sharing my journey through my darkest hours with others will help one other person in any of the many ways that so many others have helped me. This is my personal invitation to you to share my journey.

Chapter 1

Resources

Never memorize anything you can find in a book.
—*Albert Einstein*

If there is one thing my life experience has taught me, it is that no one escapes challenges. Natural disasters, cancer, war, and substance abuse are but a few examples of the many life-changing events that we are all touched by at one point or another, whether directly or indirectly through a loved one. The financial crisis of 2008 touched millions of people both directly and indirectly, and in ways that most probably thought they were immune to. Challenges like these carry with them the potential to destroy people, families, companies, countries, and cultures. From my vantage point, the only difference between those who became better people from having had experienced these challenges and those who were diminished by them was the possession of resources.

If it were not for the countless resources at my disposal and my willingness to both pursue and accept those resources, I surely would not be writing these pages. Loved ones, friends, strangers who became friends, books (oh so many books), unemployment insurance, and the food bank are just a few of those resources. The most important things I discovered about resources were that I was never alone and that there was no point in recreating the wheel. These two concepts are the foundation of what allowed me to move from a place of want to a place of abundance.

I utilize the resource of books heavily. How many times have well-intentioned friends or experts recommended a book that was helpful to them? When someone recommends a book to me, I check it out. It is amazing how many times a book has come into my life at just the right time to tell me just what I needed to know. I have even acquired books that I immediately shelved because I never made the time to read them. Then suddenly, at just the right time, the urge prompts me to read them, and they turn out to be just what I needed at that time. Throughout my story, I tell of countless times that I was in a particular emotional place, and someone recommended a book; I have included the books that have most impacted me throughout my journey these last five years in the appendix, categorized by which chapter of my journey they apply to, for your reference.

For me, books are just like people sharing with people; the only difference is that they are once removed. When a friend shares, I can look them in the eye, read their body language, and share an intimate handshake or hug. When authors share, they are trying to do exactly the same thing, but they are able to reach far more people than they otherwise could by personal sharing alone. That is exactly what I am doing right now.

Many people like me are also impacted in significant ways by music, art, ballet, opera, and theater. The media of the arts reinforce that I am not alone. I share intimately with others by participating with them in this format, and they in turn become a resource for me.

I have come to believe that I was created to need people. Truth be told I am convinced we all are but that is your personal journey, so I will leave that up to you. All I know is that I have seen the mighty power of terminal uniqueness topple many people. Some were even famous enough to make the news and enjoy the public scrutiny of their follies. In very recent times, numerous people, especially men, have fallen from this disease—countless athletes, movie personalities, rock stars, politicians, and even religious leaders. I now know my strongest ally to a life of happiness is sharing my life with someone else. Fortunately for me, throughout my journey I came to remember the importance of true friendship in the development of my thinking, choices, and actions.

Prior to my last marriage, I was well connected with a group of other men. We met at least once per week with the common goal of supporting each other in our journeys to grow and become better men, fathers, husbands, employees, employers, and community leaders. We learned from each other and held each other accountable. Somewhere along the line, however, I lost this connection. Maybe I became too enmeshed in my relationship with the opposite sex. Maybe I thought I was better. Maybe I just got lazy. Whatever the excuse, the loss of this resource ultimately contributed to the failure of my marriage. My thinking unknowingly became distorted, and my choices and actions were not far behind.

This was the kind of support that helped me understand that my life was out of balance. Maybe I was working too many hours, maybe my hobby had consumed me, or maybe I needed to eat better, exercise or sleep more. Perhaps I was in need of someone whom I respected to tell me that my wife or children needed more of me. This was how I kept my head on straight, how I got the most out of life-by participating in it with other people who were trying to do the same thing.

In my personal experience, I have seen women be far better at this concept than men. I have seen women organically grow cells of support for themselves. But as a man, I have had to work hard at it. As a man, I have had to get over the socialization deprivation that I was indoctrinated with from birth and that was reinforced on the playground and athletic field. I have had to come to grips with the reality that I need to establish healthy, honest, transparent relationships with other men in order to be successful in relationships with the opposite sex. Even though I knew this, I had not practiced these principles; I had reverted to the all-to-familiar "John Wayne" mentality most boys were taught by our self-reliant fathers.

In addition, at one time I had surrounded myself with a small circle of close friends for which I was willing to say anything to or do anything for. These few were men I admired and aspired to be like because of what they were to their families, wives, children, employees, employers, and community. But again, through nothing other than my own laziness, I lost contact with these men. I isolated myself into my own way of thinking and, by doing so, did not have to justify my actions to myself anymore.

These were not men with perfect lives—quite the contrary. In fact, these were men who shared my challenging circumstances and situations. They were ordinary men who were living life in extraordinary ways. These were men who had sharp tools because they had helped to sharpen each other's. They were man enough to hug me when I needed a hug, or simply because they were glad to see me—but they were also man enough to call me on my stupid thinking. These were men of God, and I miss you, John, Rick, and Ray.

I choose these associates very carefully because they were the inner circle of my support group. These were the men who were willing to live a life of utter transparency and brutal honesty with each other. They were the friends I could tell my deepest darks secrets to and know I would still be accepted—corrected, but accepted. These were the men I would take a call from in the middle of the night because their son was just arrested again, their teenage daughter just got pregnant, or their wife was just diagnosed with cancer, and they need someone with whom they could be honest about how they felt. They were the men that kept each other from making the headlines because of their distorted thinking, choices, behaviors, and actions. These were the men that every man needs as a resource in his life.

As a result of this journey, I have a renewed and heightened realization of just how important a role the brotherhood of a few good men has in determining the quality of another man's life. I have therefore taken it upon myself to recreate myself and create my own reality. I have taken the initiative to create a new group like this. I have extended my hand to create the inner circle, and I have offered myself as the resource to those who dare walk the road less traveled with me. I have found that when I receive a gift of humanity, the only way to keep it is to give it away.

Without getting sidetracked into a gender discussion, I have emphasized the importance of this resource for a man because I am a man, and because the women in my personal experience don't seem to have the same kinds of issues and obstacles creating this reality for themselves. In no way does this diminish the importance of this resource for women as well. I have also seen personal friends who happen to be women fall prey to the same distorted thinking, choices, behaviors, and actions as men do when they isolate themselves; the most common type is accepting mistreatment from men. I wish that all women at least have the resources in their lives to combat this one travesty.

Another valuable resource I found in this time was professional help. From the divorce lawyer to the bankruptcy attorney to the doctor, each played an invaluable role in leading me through my personal journey. My experience taught me that as much as my ego did not want to have to rely on outside sources, there were specialists that knew a lot more than I did about what choices I had. Again, too many John Wayne movies make it an extraordinary decision process for the male to solicit help, get directions, or read the manual. I have recently witnessed men younger than me die, perhaps preventively, because they could not or would not see a doctor.

Specifically, the role of the psychotherapist played a major part in assessing the end of the marriage I had vowed before God was a lifetime commitment. The divorce process itself seems to be engineered to inflame blame and guilt. The reality for me when all was said and done was that we both did the best we could with what we had, and I wish her the best, as I hope she does me. This single truth allowed me to move into the next phase of my life with forgiveness and grace, free of anger, resentment, or guilt. Every day, I witness so many people that are stuck in thinking and attitudes over previous relationships, and in reality they are only hurting themselves, preventing any forward movement into happiness and fulfillment.

Monday, September 29, 2008—this is the morning that over fifty thousand employees of Washington Mutual came to work, turned on their computers, and were redirected to a new home page with a letter explaining that they were now all employees of JPMorgan Chase. It has come to be known as the biggest bank failure in history. I was one of those employees. We learned over the next few days that the massive branch network would become an integral part of the JPMC retail footprint, but the five thousand of us at the corporate office would all be displaced over the next few months.

The FDIC guarantees your deposits at a bank when it fails, but they do not guarantee your investments. Many employees, including me, had stock in WaMu when it failed. Just like all the other investors, many of which were pension plans for other companies' employees, the WaMu employees lost their investments. In fact, the company compensated management with and encouraged investment of company stock. Many smart people were actually *buying* stock in the last days at its low price, utterly convinced it would rebound and pay off huge dividends.

Needless to say, with the loss of my job, my retirement, the breakup of my marriage, and the burden of debt bearing down on me, I had no option left but to file bankruptcy. My story of 2008 is not unique; it is now told by millions across America. My only hope is that those millions of others like me have come to a place where they realize that although they are not proud of these actions, they are culpable for their part in their own decisions and are not ashamed because, like me, they did the best they could with what they had at the time.

Unfortunately the right resources are not always available at the right time for everyone. I include these stories because they are shared by over ten million households across the nation. The experiences are very emotionally charged and controversial for even more millions who have indirectly been impacted by rising unemployment, falling home values, and diminishing investments throughout the financial crisis of 2008. Herein lays my personal experiences with the lack of resources to respond to the great recession.

Before my yacht was repossessed, I tried to sell it. The value of my pleasure craft was dropping faster than home values in 2008. It quickly slid from being worth 20 percent more than what I owed the bank too being worth less than what I owed the bank.

Since so many people found themselves in this position *"under-water"* became a common term in the media. In 2008 I had a buyer that was willing to pay fair market value, but that was only 80 percent of what I owed. I contacted the bank, and they were not willing to accept a short sale. Instead, they repossessed the craft and auctioned it off in 2009 for 30 percent of what I owed; they then proceeded with collections on me for the balance. Today, National City Bank does not exist.

In like fashion, my home had plunged in market value from 20 percent equity to underwater in just one year. After I moved out of the home and into my own apartment to begin separation and divorce proceedings, my ex-wife attempted to contact GMC Mortgage about obtaining one of the restructured loans that were supposedly available from the now infamous "Wall Street Bail Out" TARP money that the Bush administration orchestrated for the banking institution. No one would even answer the phone or return a phone call until she was in serious default of the loan, and then she was told that she did not qualify for a restructured loan on her income alone. The bank auctioned my home off for 30 percent of its appraised value two years later, and of course the bank immediately initiated legal proceedings against me for the balance. Today GMAC Mortgage does not exist.

Not to be outdone, I owed large balances on multiple credit cards, due to no one's fault but my own. However, when the financial crisis of 2008 hit, one by one my creditors began a self-destructive pattern of behavior. First they raised the interest rates, and then they raised the monthly amount due, making it impossible for me to meet these financial obligations. Then they closed the accounts from any future activity. When I would call to try and renegotiate the payments, they would demand full payment on the spot. I was not able to make doubled monthly payments, and so I surely could not make payment in full. Each account was ultimately turned over to collections.

My favorite story of all is the one of the Lexus being repossessed. The Lexus was on a lease that expired in 2008. My ex-wife approached a relative who managed a Lexus dealership about financing the residual balance at a lower monthly payment that she could both qualify for and afford on her income. At the relative's dismay, Lexus turned down the offer, and even though he already had a car lot of repossessed cars he could not sell, Lexus repossessed this one too and immediately initiated legal proceedings against me for the balance.

The financial markets' continued insistence throughout the financial crisis that nothing is better than something continues to baffle me. The mentality that auctioning collateral at ten cents on the dollar is better than accepting an 80 percent short sale is troublesome to say the least. Particularly as a lifelong corporate finance bank employee, I do not find these policies rational; in fact they seem nothing more than punitive at the expense of the economic health of an entire country, if not the world economy.

Meanwhile back at WaMu, as Chase gave out each employee's end of service notice, we were invited to participate in an outplacement service they provided. As

I stand here today, I have no hesitation saying that this resource was the single greatest thing Chase did for these five thousand people. It is unfortunate that for countless unknown reasons, only one-half of those people chose to take advantage of this great resource. I know now that the people I met and grew to know in the career center became one of the strongest influences in the direction my journey took and its subsequent outcome. I will share many more stories about my experience with the people in this outplacement service, but suffice to say here that I know of countless people who did not choose to participate in or apply this resource to their challenge, and today they are unnecessarily suffering in part from that single choice.

The outplacement service consisted of a dozen professional career experts. There were recruiters, coaches, consultants, facilitators, and development minds. Each member of the team brought his or her own unique flare and view for the multitude of people that came for assistance in this career transition, during the most difficult financial time since the Great Depression. I was fortunate enough to work with and get to know each one of them. These people touched my life in a very special way as I worked with them to apply the principals they taught to my personal journey. Even though this was a diverse cast of characters, they operated in my life as one consolidated source of energy, and so through the remainder of this book I will refer to them collectively and affectionately as "my coach."

I remember vividly showing up for my first day at this outplacement service to meet my coach. She stroked my ego by telling me I had strong experience and a good resume. Then she hit me with one of the most devastating blows of my new journey: she told me I was going to have to network to land my next job. She may as well have told me that I had terminal cancer or that I would need to learn Chinese in thirty days, because both ideas were equally mortifying to me. The thought of the term *networking* conjured up negative images of high-pressure sales and cold calling for me. I put in my time by sitting through a core curriculum of resume writing and interview skills classes over the next few weeks so that I could say that I did it with a "been there, done that" attitude. I was present but silently checked out, unwilling to accept the daunting task put before me.

At the end of each employee's service to the transition of work from WaMu to Chase, we received a retention bonus for being willing to dedicate ourselves to the transition and to not seek new employment. This arrangement brought many people many different experiences. There were those who felt guilty for the sum of money being offered in relationship to what they were contributing to the transition. There were those who gladly collected the transition pay but did not contribute as they had agreed to do. And there were those who were disgruntled by the arrangement that others were asked to stay on longer than them and receive more money than them.

This arrangement was a thorny proposition. It meant that if you were asked to remain on the payroll for six months, then you were contractually obligated to, or you would lose you retention bonus. You did not have the option of negotiating five months or seven months. You were required to accept or decline their terms, but *they* were allowed to change their terms. If they contracted you for six months, at the end of three months they could simply say, "Oops, we changed our mind." Or at the end of the six months they could say, "Just kidding—we actually need you for nine months." This was not a "pay as you go" proposition. The pay was only at the end of the contract, and only if you were still there at the end of the contract. If you did not agree to their terms, then you did not get the bonus.

What it all came down to was that if you accepted their terms, then you could not look for a new job because you never knew when you would be available to start a new job. With the high unemployment rate, this was a handicap one could not afford. I interviewed for a new job, of which I was one of the final two candidates in the running, when I received my retention offer. I was staring a lot of money in the face that I would have to decline if I accepted this new job, so I withdrew my application for the new job. Was this a dumb move or smart move? That is the question that thousands of people were asking themselves.

For me, I had agreed to stay on for nine months. When the nine months was over and the check came, it was a healthy sum of money (along with an unhealthy tax). Again, just like all the other WaMu employees, I had important decisions to make about this money. By now my finances were in a shambles: My home was in foreclosure. The yacht and Lexus had long been repossessed, and I owed thousands on credit cards. Chase had dumped five thousand people into the Seattle market over the previous nine months. Should I try to salvage what was left of my credit, or should I save the money in case it took me longer than in the past to find a new job? These were all tough questions that each of us had to answer personally.

I saw people scoop up real estate for a song and invest in rental homes. I saw people buy new cars, I saw people remodel, and I saw people put it all under a mattress. I chose a very controversial option that, in hindsight, was the perfect choice for the journey before me. Others who have not walked in my shoes hold judgment against it, and I bless you for your own view of reality. I took the money, and I went to Maui for a month. I walked away from what would have made but a dent in my financial responsibilities. I turned away from the trappings of predicting the future and financially protecting myself against the job market, and I took a vacation to enjoy, reflect, and recharge. This was the first good choice I had made in taking care of myself that I can remember.

My trip to Maui turned out to be a manifestation of the journey I was now on, but I did not realize it yet. This was my first time off the North American continent. It was one of many choices to come about doing what I wanted with my life, and it was truly a spiritual experience. Everything from the local people to the geography to the climate spoke to me like an ancient sage. New experiences like surfing, swimming with the turtles, and boating with a school of dolphin were all incensed by a connection with the universe and my place in this creation. The sunsets on the warm water, the peaceful crash of the surf throughout the night accompanying the warm tropical rain, and the refreshing sunrise inspired me to reconstruct my disastrous life. It was clearly one of the most blessed months of my life.

I have always been a water person. The feeling of it surrounding my skin, the feeling of weightlessness when I am in it, the childlike behavior that grown adults revert to when they are in it—it has always captivated me. Even though I had a serious knee injury at the time, I was not going to pass up the opportunity to learn how to surf. I had never gotten any closer to it than watching it in a movie, but I had always wanted to experience it. I knew that the professionally paid extreme sportsmen on the north shore would laugh at me, but the thrill of simply learning how to stand up on the board in four feet of water and ride what was more of a tide than a wave into shore was beyond words. I wanted to do it over and over again. I wanted deeper water and bigger waves. I had the bug. But even the simple beginnings took its toll on my knee, so I compromised by spending hours frolicking in the surf with my little body board.

Of particular significance was the day I went swimming with the turtles in Maui. I went with a small group of other tourists in kayaks. There was one instance when I got separated from the group. While I was away from the noise, I lay still in the shallow water and encountered a single turtle that was as large as me. Suspended under water, the two of us slowly and methodically investigated each other; neither of us was afraid or anxious. I was so close that I could see his eyes. I could read the growths and markings on his shell. I felt connected there in silence with him. This moment seemed to last a day. Then he slowly turned and gently paddled away. I shall never forget it; it was a deeply spiritual experience for me to harmonize with one of God's other creatures.

On another occasion I chartered a boat to go snorkeling at Molokini. We had hours to bob on the surface of the most clear water I had seen, gazing deep into a sea of multiple species and colors of fish. The colors were the most startling, brilliant colors I had ever seen. It was breathtaking and exhilarating. With a little practice and coordination, I could hold my breath and dive down a reasonable distance and get an even closer view of the underwater life. I did so several times and was so entranced that I nearly forgot to come up for air.

As if this time near this remote island was not enough, on our way back we attracted a school of dolphin. Apparently dolphins love riding the bow wake, the trough of water pushed in front of a moving boat, because the water around the bow of the boat creates a low pressure system. This not only provides a perfect place to surf, have fun, and play, but it also allows them to get pushed by the boat and be able to travel long distances effortlessly. Whatever the scientific explanation, this was a delight to observe.

I spent most of my downtime in Maui trying to figure out how I could stay there and make a living without having to work two or three minimum-wage jobs like most people do to afford the cost of living there. I had fallen in love. At the end of my month in paradise, I returned home bleached blond, tan, and revitalized by the warm climate, culture, and experience. I had made an investment in me that is paying dividends to this day. I honestly believe there does not exist a stronger investment for the return than this trip was for me. This experience gave me the fortitude that I would need to enter into the upcoming darkest, lowest part of my life.

When I returned to Seattle, my new bliss was short lived. Just like so many times in the past, I had a swift round of interviews with a handful of employers where I was absolutely convinced I was a shoe-in . . . but this time they were all falling through. In short time I came to realize this market was different, and it was going to be very hard to get a new job at the income level to which I was accustomed. I started receiving unemployment benefits, but it was not enough to pay basic bills. I quickly ran out of money, could not pay my bills, and ultimately received an eviction notice from the apartment I was renting. Had I done the right thing with the money? Should I have . . . ? Could I have . . . ? None of that mattered now. I had created my own reality, and now I was sitting in it.

Once again resources became a survival tool for me during this time. The first step I had to take was to acknowledge how unmanageable my life had become (realize I needed help). The next step I had to take was to swallow my pride and let my friends know about my situation (reach out for help). I immediately had gracious people offering me odd jobs to make ends meet, and I utilized the services of the food bank to eat. The final of the first three steps to being able to breathe again was being willing to do whatever it took to get a job again. Now God had me right where he wanted me, and it didn't feel good at all—in fact it was miserable.

It was during this time that I returned to the outplacement service with my tail between my legs. I was now willing to listen, learn, and apply whatever it took to get me out of a situation that was painful financially, emotionally, psychologically, mentally, and physically. I was financially and emotionally broke and bankrupt. I was psychologically wrapped around an axle, and I was mentally tortured. Physically I was at the breaking point that I had witnessed in others when the mind, spirit, and soul are not cooperating, and their body suffers from the turmoil.

In my case, I had been physically suffering from chronic osteoarthritis since high school; I will go deeper into that in a later chapter. For now, I was on my hands and knees pulling weeds in my friends' lawns so that I could pay rent, and I was in excruciating pain. Again I made my plight known to those in my inner circle, and lo and behold some other friends conspired to find me some odd jobs working at a desk. This work alleviated the pain and provided the monetary means to stave off an eviction notice from my landlord while I continued to look for gainful employment.

In my lowest moment, God was beginning to show me that he was in charge and that his resources were limitless. Above all, this has been my life lesson from this journey.

All abundance and prosperity are of God. It rains on the just and the unjust alike. God continues to place this message in front of my wondering, weary eyes from Jeremiah 29:11. "'For I know the plans I have for you,' declares the Lord, 'plans to prosper you and not to harm you, plans to give you hope and a future.'"

Everyone has resources. No matter who you are or what position you are in, you have resources. Admitting that you need resources, knowing that you have resources, and being willing to utilize resources is the difference between hopelessness and hope. You may be feeling hopeless, but you are not helpless. Ask for help and be amazed. I did, and I was.

Chapter 2

Fear

"The only thing we have to fear is fear itself."
—*Franklin D. Roosevelt*

False evidence appearing real: this is F.E.A.R. Nothing more, nothing less. Fear is what prevents us from utilizing resources.

Let me start out by explaining some important, self-professed terminology so that you can understand the meaning of these terms as I use them throughout the remainder of this book. The First term is Mentor. To me, a mentor is someone who teaches you. The mentor challenges you, questions you, resists you, weakens you, and hopes you respond. The second term is sage. For me a sage is someone from whom you learn. The sage welcomes you and empowers you. The sage accepts you as you are and does not instruct but offers personal experience. The mentor is like the closed fist; the sage is like the open palm. Both the mentor and the sage have their places. I would hope that all people have both a mentor and a sage in their lives, as I do. You should have a mentor to challenge you and a sage to guide you.

However, just as I explained about my coaches in the career center, my mentor and sage are not actually just one person but a collection of my inner circle who act as one in my life's journey. In addition all of my coaches, mentors and sage are not gender specific in reality, but I will refer to them as her or him to further emphasize the polar opposite roles they played in my journey. I make this distinction in my life whether or not it is universally true because I have in my life a sage. He is my sage simply because he has what I want. Sometimes he happens to be older than I am, and sometimes he is younger. He has walked through my challenges in a way that I want to, with the results that I want. My sage has never told me what to do. I share, he shares, and I know what to do. That works for me.

I would like to explore another term that floats around: character defects. I don't believe there is such a thing. God has made each of us a unique character (in more ways than one). Each of us is unique in our character, and therefore our unique character is our perfect us. On the other hand, we willingly make choices and decisions, adopting thinking and feelings that diminish our God-given character and uniqueness. Until such a time that these blemishes are cleared up, we have created for ourselves "defects of character."

Now, back to fear. My sage believes that all defects of our God-designed characters are based in fear; by recognizing and facing our fears, we realign ourselves to our true selves. Anger, sadness, resentment, and depression are but a few of the multitude of feelings that can rush through me as I go through any given day, and they are all rooted in fear. My sage referred me to a prominent author named Susan Jeffries, who handles this concept better than anyone else I have read. I will not attempt to reproduce her principles here, but I will tell you that her books have had a tremendous impact on my ability to recognize, face, overcome, and diminish my fears. Much of my frustration comes from my unwillingness to accept what I cannot change. Much of my fear comes from my inability to force a solution to my problems.

Though understanding and dealing with fear may make me uncomfortable, I know it is an important part of my journey. When I allow myself to appreciate the full range of feelings, I come to realize that fear serves me in many important ways. It lets me know when I have been hurt or mistreated. It might be signaling me to respond differently to a person or situation. Often my fear reminds me to take better care of myself. Facing my fears helps me deal with my issues such as grief, frustration, and loneliness. When I courageously and carefully examine where I am, the door to change is opened.

To me, Susan Jeffries's most important point is that fear is a natural, God-given response. It is my fear that protects me from harm in times of real danger, as it should. But fear of perceived danger from distorted thinking is what prevents me from growing and living a fulfilling life. Identifying and walking through my fears was the scariest and most profitable part of my journey that continues to empower me to find my proper place in this world. When I face my fear, it loses its power; when it loses its power it, loses its grip on me.

So many of us never learn how to recognize our own feelings and understand where they come from, let alone track the secondary emotion back to the root fear and face it. I know that when I first met my sage, I could not tell you how I felt about anything, let alone how I felt at any given moment. I was in survival mode and was completely numb. While working with him, I learned what I wanted, how I felt, what I was afraid of, and how to face it. Today I am much more in touch with myself, what drives me, and how to steer in a different direction, but it still takes me much more time and energy to process it then he needs, because he has had more practice at it. I now know that no one else can control my emotions. No one can make me angry, sad, or happy without me giving them permission to do so. My feelings are my own. I am responsible for my own feelings, no one else is. I am never responsible for anyone else's feelings.

My sage told me of a wonderful example of this concept. He shared a story of a day when he was meditating and had a very vivid vision. In the vision he was walking through a jungle and came upon an opening to a cave, but the cave was guarded by a ferocious dragon. He wanted into the cave, but he knew the only way into it was through the dragon. He closed his eyes and walked straight toward the opening to the cave—and directly into the dragon. In doing so, he reached the inside of the cave to realize the dragon was never really there; it had only been his imagination. As he entered the cave, he found an amazingly beautiful oasis of gardens and waterfalls, which he stayed in and enjoyed. As he departed from the cave entrance out which he had entered, he now understood that he was free to return and enjoy this sacred place, experiencing it at any time he wished without fear of the dragon.

That September day in 2008, when fifty thousand WaMu employees came to their first day of work as Chase employees, my manager at WaMu called his department together to talk through everyone's understanding of what had just happened, what was going to happen, and how everyone felt about it. At the time this was not terribly upsetting to me. I have now been through nine employment displacements throughout my career. Personally, in the long run I had always gotten a better job out of the deal, so I was not all too concerned. But my manager was angry, and my peers visibly displayed signs of shock and fear. Emotions were high that morning, and none of us had a clue of just how bad things were about to get.

I tried to share what I thought was sage wisdom at the time; my manager even thanked me for my perspective. But people only hear what they are ready and willing to hear, and nobody was in the mood to hear much of anything that day. They were scared, nervous, and twitchy. They were dazed and confused and in shock. They were grasping for what they were going to tell their wives and children, who undoubtedly had already heard the news on the TV or radio. Some family members, like mine, were already calling and e-mailing, looking for explanations and reassurances.

There was no work done that day at what had been the headquarters to WaMu in Seattle. Men and women in suits and skirts stepped out of town cars and into the pristine tower that had showcased WaMu's success. They may as well have had big signs on their foreheads that read, "New York." They stuck out like sore thumbs among the thousands of business-casual WaMu employees. They were swift and direct; they came, they conquered, and they left. We, stood dazed and confused, didn't even know what had hit us.

Nearly five years later, I know of thousands of people who sat in meetings across the company just like this one, and many are still stuck in their anger and fear. There are those who got new jobs, some very quickly, but they hate their jobs because they have never processed their anger. There are those that still do not have jobs and are still being controlled by their fears. There are divorces, foreclosures, and bankruptcies, like mine. There are illnesses, diseases, depression, and even suicide over the events that unfolded at 1301 Second Avenue on September 29, 2008.

As I was processing my own divorce, foreclose, repossessions, and loss of retirement fund over the ensuing months, I also watched as the employee base in the WaMu center dwindled when I came to work each day. Every day, another person was cleaning out their desk, turning in the equipment, backing up their personal items and saying their goodbyes. First I saw the pictures of kids, calendars of wiener dogs, and posters of Huskies come down from the cubicle walls, and then I saw the faces of those I had done battle with disappear. Each day the space on my floor became more empty, and I could see fewer heads sitting at their desks.

It was grief beyond sadness. I wandered to other floors in the building to see who was still there each day, and I found no relief. Floor after floor of the forty-two-story building reflected the same decimation. As the employee base dwindled, so did the dress, posture, faces and attitudes of those who remained on to personally witness and experience the painful, drawn-out death of a once great financial institution. These people experienced the full range of emotions associated with all the hard work, dedication, and investment that each person had personally contributed toward the company. Those who were able to process this loss through all the stages of the grieving process were few and fortunate.

As I walked into the building each morning and left each evening, I also took notice of the slowly dwindling business community that surrounded the WaMu center.

First, the coffee stations equipped with cups, coffee, tea, sugar, cream, and a cold water fountain were no longer maintained or stocked, next, the neighborhood cafes that we had on several floors of the building disappeared, and then the employee cafeteria that occupied half of the sixteenth floor was closed. I could walk right up to the counter of the Starbucks in the lobby that had once maintained a long stream of faithful constituents all day long. The small variety store on the other side of the floor, where one could purchase a lottery ticket or last-minute greeting card, went out of business.

Around the block and down the street, small businesses, restaurants, sandwich shops, coffee shops, and variety stores that survived off of the five thousand employees of WaMu disappeared over night. With no employees to purchase their goods and services, these businesses died the same slow, anguishing death that WaMu did. As I walked by the now empty buildings, I could not help but wonder about them and the families that these businesses had supported. How did they go home and explain to their wives and their children that their American dream had been shattered, too? Were they losing their homes and cars too? Were their once happy homes disrupted with resentful children? Were they able to process their sadness and anger? Did they overcome their fears? It was estimated that for every WaMu employee who lost his or her job, another 2.5 people in the

The Fall of My Life

downtown business district lost theirs too. It was a dark, heavy, *unbearable time.*

For me, the life lesson about fear is that it was holding me back—or at least, I did not recognize or understand that my feelings were holding me back. Not recognizing or understanding my fears was crippling me. One of the first things my sage asked me was, "What is your biggest fear?" Without blinking I was able to answer. Unlike a lot of people and most of my family, I am not afraid of dying; I have made peace with my maker, and I am ready to meet him. My biggest fear was of dying alone and being one of those people that one reads about in the news—the ones that are found dead in a rent-controlled apartment by the landlord because a neighboring tenant complained that the smell of the decomposing body was so bad. No one knew these people were dead but no one missed them. In my opinion, this is life's biggest tragedy, and it is what I feared the most. I was creating my own reality and attracting everything I did not want.

I am happy to report that this is no longer a fear of mine. In fact, I recently reported to my sage that now my biggest fear is that first sip of chai tea in the morning, the one where I carefully sip it because I do not know how full the cup is or how hot it is. I never know if it is going to burn my tongue. He replied with a loving response: "If that is your biggest fear, then you have come a long way."

A long way is a long, painful, scary journey, and I do not think there are any shortcuts. Indulge me to walk through my journey with you, and then at least maybe yours will be better lit.

Let me clarify that I am a strong advocate of psychotherapy, but I think it is highly misunderstood. People's ignorance makes it the brunt of a lot of jokes on late-night comedy routines and in movies. My experience is that there is immense power in understanding my childhood interactions with adults and other children, but I can't stop there or else I will get stuck there—still in my childhood, still with my childhood issues. The power resides in taking responsibility for my perceptions and ensuing decisions then and now, regardless of the behavior, actions, and attitudes of anyone else. Childhood fears can be the most complicated fears of all and the hardest to overcome, but I think it was one of the most important things I had to do to recover from the WaMu grief and to move on to a better place and a better me.

I like to call it making "remakes" instead of "reruns." As one example, I had an older brother who was dethroned as the baby when I was born. He subsequently made it his life's mission to make my life miserable. He physically, verbally, emotionally, mentally, and physiologically tortured me until he left home for college. I was well into adulthood before I understood that he was just doing the best he could with what he had at the time. My brother and I never became good friends, but my forgiveness and acceptance of his imperfections allowed us to share many treasured bonding moments around what we *did* have in common before he passed away. I faced my biggest childhood fear and have reaped the benefits.

In this example, today I can hear a criticizing remark that sparks the same feelings my brother may have aroused forty-five years ago, and I have a choice. I can choose to feel like I did when I was nine and behave the way I did when I was nine; this is like rerunning the same old movie over and over yet expecting a different ending. Or I can choose to not be nine anymore, accept this new criticism with the same forgiveness and acceptance that I granted my brother, and remake the ending to my new movie. The latter is a lot more gratifying. I do not have to allow my fear to control me anymore. I have the power to create my own new reality because I have let go of the past that was holding me back and keeping me captive.

The healing part of facing your fear is in letting go. There is a natural order to the universe, and when I let go of a fear, I allow this natural order to unfold and open myself up to new ways of thinking, making decisions, behaving, and acting. When I let go of a fear, I am affirming my right to live my life on my terms, to make my own choices, and to grow as I experience the results of those choices. My obsessive interference with the natural order disrupts my connection with my own spiritual self.

Also, in my family of six there was another devastating childhood disease: non-communication. I am here to say that the most intense loneliness is found within a home in which there is no communication. Walled-off hearts between family members can create an agonizing sense of loneliness, which is often the result of a closed heart. Our fear of being hurt, rejected, or judged keeps us frozen in our loneliness. In that place of pain and blame, we become psychologically numb to our feelings and the feelings of others; we can't feel pain, fear, loneliness, or empathy.

When we let go of the fear and pain and open ourselves to others, the loneliness disappears. Our hearts are healed only through loving, caring, opening, sharing, helping, giving, feeling, embracing, and warming the universe with our love. But beware—constant activity in the outside world without the balance of inner activity contributes to our loneliness. We end up separating ourselves from the very thing that gives us peace. Slow down and listen to the voice within that connects us all.

Many times I have dreaded broaching a certain subject because I knew it would be difficult to talk about it. Maybe that's because it feels awkward, or because I know the loved one or coworker will bristle when addressed. But I know I have to get it over with, and the sooner the better. I have learned that I am probably magnifying the problem in my mind and that my imagination is taking over. When I finally did muster up the courage, it really wasn't as difficult as I had feared—but I had to take that first step.

In my family, no one discussed or displayed emotions or feelings. I never knew where I stood, good or bad; no affection was shown. Secrets, resentment, and un-forgiveness abounded. The word *"LOVE"* was never spoken—and I mean never. Everything was superficially happy until it wasn't; I felt loved until I didn't. I had food, shelter, and clothing, but I was never nourished. I often joke with my close friends now, "My excuse is I was raised by wolves. What's yours?"

Not surprisingly, when I hit puberty, if you were a girl and you liked me, then I loved you. This disastrous thinking negatively impacted all my relationships well into adulthood. I was a self-proclaimed bachelor, but I married my junior year in college to a girl with whom I was head over heels in love. She was everything I was not. She was confident, extraverted, and outspoken. She came from a strong spiritual family, and she loved her father. We were good friends, enjoyed each other's company, and shared common interests and political and spiritual views. She left me shortly after we graduated from college with the parting message that she had never loved me. She added that she had married me because our friends and family thought she should. She knew how much I loved her, so she had tried to love me, like an arranged marriage, but she could no longer pretend. I was clueless she had ever harbored such feelings, and I was devastated. The mixed blessing was that it was her idea for us to move to Seattle; this was the backdrop where my lifelong work on myself began.

I have heard of so many people that have been married multiple times. How many keep marrying the same person over and over again but with a different name, because they sincerely believe that the other person is always the problem? They are never honest enough with themselves to consider that they at least contribute to the problems. I was determined to not be one of those people. I needed to know why I had been so clueless. I wanted to know what it was that I didn't know. I longed to understand why other people seemed to have loving relationships, but I was not capable of finding one.

I will say that I never did buy into the lie that I was somehow not lovable; I knew this to not be true. I say this because I know that millions get stuck on this reality. Somehow they bestow upon themselves the folly of the people that have injured them. They take on the fault and become ashamed. They confuse who they are with what has happened. They refuse to understand that they are a perfect child of God and that God loves them just the way they are. They deny themselves the dignity and respect that was taken from them by those in whom they had placed misguided trust. They think themselves to be unlovable. It saddens me to meet these people. It angers me to see how a predator can easily wreak havoc on another person's life.

I enjoyed a few years of introspective bachelor life. I saw multiple coaches and read multiple self-help books in my relentless pursuit to grasp the secrets to love that had eluded me. Then the day came. I was ready to marry again. I remarried in my late twenties to a lady with three little girls aged four, six, and eight. Their biological father was AWOL, so although the juvenile court system would not allow me to legally adopt them, I did so in every sense of the term, raising these three girls over the next ten years.

Two years later we gave birth to my only biological child, a boy who had my likeness. I had the great fortune of being in the delivery room when my son was born. Child birth is an indescribable miracle. I held my son as the doctor severed the umbilical cord, and I washed the amniotic fluid off his body. I weighed him, measured him, took his footprints, and wrapped him in his first blanket under the direction of the nurse in charge. I still believe a bond that cannot be broken was formed in those first few impressionable minutes of his life.

Not long after the birth of my son, my marriage turned into a battleground of nonstop fighting and arguing that went through the same vicious circle each time. Concerned neighbors who could hear the fighting called the police. Friends intervened to help. We both exhausted every resource at our disposal to change the way we interacted with each other. In the middle of one of our doozies, I found my young son face down on his bed with a pillow over his head and his hands over his ears, so that he could not see or hear the fight. My spirit was crushed—this had to stop. Through the persistence of friends, I ended this union. I had done everything I knew how to, but it was not enough. I had not figured out this marriage thing. I did not yet have the tools to live in a relationship with another person.

Even though my son remained with his mother when I moved out, I took the early shift at work so that I could get off in time to pick him up every day from school and share in his academic and after-school activities, including soccer, basketball, baseball, and scouts. Each day I drove the eighty-six-mile round trip from Federal Way to Woodinville to foster my relationship with my son. After extracurricular activities, I fed him dinner and helped him with his homework. His mother and I alternated weekends with him. Whether it was her weekend or mine, I made the trek to participate in his weekend activities. I wanted my son to know that he was my number-one priority, that he was the most important thing to me.

Three years later my son came to live with me for the remainder of his school years. I now have a grown man for a son who has served his country and is able to communicate to me what he thinks and how he feels. Considering his upbringing, I could not be more proud of this young man.

The twisted fate is that upon removing myself from this marriage, I came to realize later that I had never loved this woman, just as my first wife had never loved me. I had not understood that I had married her because I fell in love with those three precious little girls of hers. I made every attempt to maintain relationships with each of these girls during and after the divorce, but contact with them quickly dwindled. My heart broke and still breaks each time I stop to contemplate what they must have gone through while living in that house. It is painful but understandable to accept why they don't want to communicate with me anymore. An opportunity to openly and honestly clear the air and restore those relationships is a gift that I do not see in my future.

I carved out a few more years of blissful bachelorhood with more counseling and more reading, and this time I even joined a men's support group. Now I had definitely arrived—I was ready to marry again and be successful at it. I remarried again in my early forties to a wonderful woman who shared my values and accepted me with all my faults. Even though I told myself I would not again enter into another mixed family marriage, I fell in love with this woman, and she had three early teenagers. We got married six months after meeting. I remember when we were still dating, one occasion on a car ride with her three kids and my son, they broke out into a song: "We Are Family." It was cute beyond cute, but it was short lived.

She quickly developed animosity toward my son, and I toward her oldest son. She created a double standard in the house between my son and her kids, and I could not tolerate that her oldest son treated her just like his father (her ex-husband) did. The problem was that I stored all that anger and frustration up inside of me because I was bound and determined that there would be no fighting in this house—and there was not. At the time I was never sure what my true feelings were, but I knew I was dying on the inside. The unspoken, unresolved, pent-up guilt and resentment was eating me up and ultimately threw me into the bowels of what I now know to be a self-destructive affair subconsciously designed to get me caught and provide justification for the way out of my self-imposed captivity. I ended life commitment number three, which took an unnecessary toll on innocent hearts.

My wife's ex-husband was actively involved in the lives of their three children, and they shared joint custody. Even though I could never find a way to connect with either of the boys, I did form a special bond with her daughter; I came to think of and treat her as one of my own. She was away at college when I moved out of the house. My actions were especially devastating to her. She called me and texted me for quite some time, begging me to reconcile with her mother. If only there was a way to end a relationship without collateral damage. To my son's credit, he maintains a healthy relationship with all of his half-sisters and step siblings to this day. I don't know where he got that talent.

In addition to my three marriages, there were a handful of women in between my marriages that I would have easily married if not for the fact that they were too smart to marry me. They had been given, or else they developed, the tools to live in a relationship, and they were able to recognize someone who was not ready. I could be charming and witty when courting, but once they got to know the real me, they knew that this was not a relationship that they could fix, and it would not last. I thank those women from the bottom of my heart for their honesty with themselves and for the motivation I received from not being able to experience them on their terms.

I am neither proud of nor ashamed of my marriages. I think this is an important distinction worth discussing. Shame is a feeling associated with who I am. I am Welch, I am tall, and I am blue eyed; these are things that I cannot control, and they are what make up Bob. Guilt is a feeling associated with a thought, behavior, action, or attitude: "I feel guilty when I talk to you like that or do that to you."

When we get the two confused, we get all crossed up. I should not feel guilty for being blue eyed, and I should not be ashamed that I spoke to you in that way, but I should feel guilty that I did.

I am not proud of the decisions I made, the thinking I did, the behaviors I chose, or the actions I initiated. But I am not ashamed because these decisions, thinking, behaviors, and actions that I feel guilty for are not of the true me. They are of a distorted, flawed me, a me that I have the choice to change, improve on, and be a better form of who I really am. My last boss, in paying me a compliment on how far I had progressed, lovingly told me that her first impression of me was that I was an angry asshole.

If I thought that this form of me was the true me and felt ashamed, I would be stuck and doomed. I have no regrets because every stupid decision has made me exactly who I am today, perfectly imperfect.

Fear in relationships now owned me. What had started out as childhood insecurity had infested my adult life like a cancer. My inability to understand and behave like an adult in relationships had now created my biggest fear. I had a fear that I would never have a meaningful relationship and that I would die alone. I know there are millions of people every year who reach this same point and give up, but there was an undeniable force in me that refused to believe a meaningful relationship was impossible.

Some of my actions were admirable and justified; others were embarrassing and inexcusable. Rationalization and justification can become our best friends and our worst enemies. I was attracted to the possibility of discovering parts of myself that I never knew existed. I explored whether my attitudes and assumptions about life were serving my best interests. I could see the way I was living my life. I got a glimpse of how control, people pleasing, fear, and other shortcomings stood in my way of my serenity. I learned that I needed to be honest, open, and willing in order to discover who I really was.

I needed the willingness to face things—some things that have haunted me from the past, and other things about myself that I may discover that I don't like. I needed the willingness to take back my power. I needed the willingness to experience long-frozen emotions, whatever they might be. I needed to be willing to try a new way. I also needed the openness to see myself differently, to drop my roles, and to look at how I had let life affect me. It would have been easier to hide and isolate, but then I never would have written this book. Each new experience lit a candle in my darkness. Each spiritual awakening added another measure of light to my life.

When I had all my material and financial securities stripped out from underneath me, I was left with the relentless nagging of what really was important to me in this short life on earth. It did not take much pondering to come to the conclusion that relationships are all that really matters in the end. I spent much energy reading and studying how I could get better at relationships. Notice that I did not say, "How do I find the right person?" or, "How do I survive without relationships?" I turned my focus to being a better me.

I found dozens of books (which I reference in my appendix) that helped me understand a key point at this point in my journey. What was holding me back? The dragon guarding the cave entrance? For me, the answer came like Seattle's cold northern winds. What was holding me back was simply that I wanted to be liked. Guess what? Everybody wants to be liked. Yes really. I know it sounds crazy, but trust me on this one: everybody wants to be liked. Now, guess what secret I unveiled? If I like someone first and know how to appropriately demonstrate it, chances are they are going to like me back. If I know what I want I can attract what I want.

Let me repeat this concept so you do not miss it. This will be on the test. Pay attention! If I want to be liked, then I reach out and like someone else. Instead of sitting around in my fear wondering why no one likes me, I get up and do something for someone else. Take baby steps. Smile at a stranger and odds are they will smile back. Then off I go. Now actually Say hi to someone and chances are they are going to say hi in return. Now that I have done it, I can do it again. Try speaking full sentences to someone, and chances are you will get a full sentence in response. At this point I am now addicted; this feels good. And the really crazy part is that what feels good is not the being liked (well, okay, that feels good too), but the liking itself. That is what drew me out and propelled me forward to serve others.

This was particularly prevalent in my job search. As I mentioned before, on my first visit with my career coach at the WaMu/Chase outplacement service, she told me I was going to have to network, and I blew her off. The way I saw it, I had two friends, and one was my dog. I was a self-made man and was not going to ask for help. I had gotten new jobs eight other times in my career without networking, and I would do it again. I would simply work harder at it. I would get a job and I would show her.

I even tried a hybrid form of "networking for chickens" for a while, because I wanted to avoid the whole concept so much. Basically, this concept consisted of applying for jobs online and then trying to get someone to help me move my resume and application through the bowels of corporate HR unscathed. After all, I knew people in the marketplace that were sure to help me. I tried this approach with hundreds on job postings during the next few months. The reality was that out of the five thousand people who once worked in WaMu headquarters, at least one thousand of them were highly educated and qualified finance people like me. I estimated that half of those people were either seeking the entry level or senior management positions I was not, which meant that for every open position I was applying for, probably five hundred former WaMu finance personnel were applying for the same job. When that got painful enough for me to try something different, I stopped trying the same thing over and over again and expecting it to change.

Six months later, I was back asking my coach, "How does this networking thing work?" As it turns out, it works just like relationships. Go figure. That is not what she actually said, and that is not what I heard at the time, but that is what I finally came to realize. To put it simply, if all I do is ask people to help me find a job in this economy, I will hear my own echo followed by the sound of crickets. Millions of people want and need a job right now. But if I make myself a resource to others, I become invaluable. I become a known commodity. I am the first thing on people's minds when they first learn of opportunities. People think of me when they know about the needs of the company before those needs translate into a job. This is effective because no one else is doing it, and I stand out from the crowd. I have differentiated myself from the hundreds of other fully qualified candidates.

The fear that I may never get a job, or at least as good a job, in the last ten years of my career was replaced by strength, power, and momentum. My attitude of "Please like me" was replaced with "Do I like you? Are you what I want in my life?" In both my personal and professional lives, I was recreating myself, and the two were not as different as they used to be. When I met new people in my personal circles, I asked myself whether this was the kind of person I wanted to attract into my life. When I interviewed, I felt a shift from trying to convince an employer to like me to making the employer convince *me* to like *them*. I do not want to spoil the ending just yet, but the job I ultimately got provided both.

I now know that my relationships can be of the quality I have been longing for all my life. I am able to kindly set boundaries that I must have for my own serenity. I do not have to give my opinion about everything others say and do or don't say and do. I have begun to honestly say things I would have held back or tried to work around before including what I think, how I feel, and what I want. I have learned how to take care of myself, and I have learned that problems do not go away by themselves. They must be worked through, or else they forever remain a barrier to the growth and development of the relationship.

Let me be perfectly clear about something. The first time I went to a networking event, I thought I was going to throw up. My palms were sweaty and I had gas. I stood in the corner and hoped no one would notice me. The room was packed with hundreds of unemployed people. I did not give a damn about any of them; I was there because my career coach told me this was how I was going to get a job, but I did not see how any of these people were going to get me a job. It was hot and claustrophobic, and I wanted to go home. I thought, *There must be a better way to do this. There must be something I don't know.*

I returned back to the career center and discussed it with my career coach, and she thought I simply needed more practice at something that did not naturally come to me. All I knew was that what I had been doing wasn't working for me, so I reluctantly and obediently tried the next scheduled networking event. The event organizer stopped us all in the middle of the event and used a little exercise to explain how to do this. He instructed everyone to pair up. Each person got one minute to deliver the elevator speech that we had all been taught to develop to perfection. Then he asked us how it went. I was shocked to hear him and everyone else describe what a miserable experience it was. I was not the only one who did not care about the person with whom I was partnered; they were all there simply to get a job, too. Then he instructed us to *never* do that again. Alternatively, he told us to be a resource. "Try your one minute again, but this time ask them what *they* are looking for and find out how you can be a resource to them." In other words, ask not what your networking event can do for you, but what you can do for your networking event. Be a resource.

Fireworks! That was the answer! That changed everything that had to do with networking for me from that day forward. I tried it, and it worked. Yes, I know people you want to know. Yes, I know things you want to know. Yes, I can help. I started a practice of asking people what they wanted, telling them I could help them, and taking their business card. After the event I would ask them to connect with me on LinkedIn, and I would invite them to coffee. At coffee I would show them how I could help, and guess what? Now I had built a relationship, and now they wanted to help me. I never had to ask for help after that day.

In short time I was looking forward to networking events. I invited others to events so that they could share my experience. I was attending two a week. I would be the first there and would find a strategic location in the middle of the room where I was accessible to everyone. I had people whom I had met at previous events bring people to me and tell them they had to meet me. I had people come to me who had been looking for me because they had heard about me. I never had to move. I stood in one place like a beacon, and they came to me. I could be a resource to all these people, and I could build relationships with them.

Why does this work? I think it is simple: everybody wants to be liked. When I ask you what you want, I listen to you tell me, and when I tell you I think I can help, I am telling you I like you. But when I am willing to be a resource, I am also telling you I like myself. When you hear me say that I like you and I like myself, then you are going to like me. The human condition simply cannot respond in any other way; it is innate. You can try to deny it, and you can resist it, but it is the truth nonetheless.

When I ask you to meet me over coffee for a chat, you are immediately suspect my motives; you agree but with reservations. What do I want? But when I tell you that all I want is for you to tell me about your job, your company, and the people in it, you hear me tell you I like you, and you spill your guts. I saw it a hundred times. People loved to talk about themselves, especially when I asked them to, and now they felt comfortable that I didn't want anything in return. If they loved their job, they wanted to me you all about it. If they hated their job, they wanted to tell me all about it.

At this point in my job search, I was having coffee (I do not actually drink coffee; I use this as a term for meeting at a coffee house to chat) at least twice a day and going to networking events at night. I was energized by all the stimulation (not the caffeine). But a very important point that I was not keenly aware of was that I was keeping myself sharp and professional by being out with other professionals all day and all night. I was not sitting at home, becoming stale, and feeling sorry for myself. I was creating my own reality, and it was responding. This was a high for me. As I learned later, this brain stimulation is from a natural, body-generated chemical called dopamine, which is the same chemical found in cocaine that gives the temporary artificial high.

I learned that I would crash after this high. I learned that just as the body generates the high, the body needs regeneration. I learned to take care of myself in this process. I have to eat right, get plenty of exercise and sleep, and practice prayer and meditation. If I do not do this, my entire system gets out of whack, and I will be of no use to anyone, including myself. If I continue to push the envelope, I will become ill. The body has an interesting way of telling me who is in charge. I listen to it. Like they say, all work and no play makes Bob a dull boy.

We have all heard the take-off instructions on the airplane that in the event of a drop in cabin pressure, air masks will deploy. The direct order is to get my own mask on first before I try to assist others. Have you ever stopped to think about why they tell you this? If I can't breathe, I can't help anybody else. Forget about everything you have ever seen in any airplane disaster movie. If I try to save everybody else without taking care of myself first, I will die. This lesson is no different in life. What is generated must be regenerated. It is a physical law of the universe that I cannot beat.

Let me detour here and destroy all your preconceived notions about prayer and meditation. This is not a sermon about "Now I lay me down to sleep" or "Lord, won't you give me a Mercedes Benz." I am referring to surrender—not to give up, but to let go. When I surrender, I drop the limiting barriers of my own past experiences and make allowances for future possibilities, possibilities that of myself, I cannot otherwise anticipate. I let go of my limited ideas of what could be and open my heart to opportunities that I might not have dreamed possible. That is what happens for me when I pray and meditate.

Just because I can't see how things are going to work out at the present moment, that doesn't mean a way won't reveal itself later. I don't have to know all the answers in advance; the answers are not my responsibility. As I let go, however, I have seen how things can be resolved seemingly on their own. Through repetition I learned to trust in the process. Over time my serenity deepened as I gained confidence that everything would turn out for the best according to a greater plan, even if I didn't understand it fully. I found peace and developed faith.

I came to see that God *cares* if I put my trust and faith in him. He *cares* if I hurt myself or others, if I carry the message of grace, hope, and love. God *cares* if I believe in him, if

I help others. He *cares* about my seemingly trivial hopes, dreams, disappointments, if I will make it or not. God *cares* if I choose to call on him. He *cares* about me and for me.

I also learned something about the term *introvert*. I have heard so many other people use the excuse that they cannot do this or that because they are introverts; I have used the excuse myself. This is a very misunderstood term that carries a lot of negative, self-defeating thinking with it. I confirmed I am an introvert, much to the surprise of those who know me today. But I learned that being an introvert does not mean what I thought it did. What it defines is not who I am but the way in which I regenerate. Introverts regenerate in private; extroverts regenerate with others. It does not mean I like to be by myself. It simply means that after being energized by being around other people, I need to regenerate on my own. Oops, there goes my excuse for not being out.

Let me stop here for a moment and clarify another important point. This is not arrogance—this is sincerity, this is intention, this is knowing and creating my own reality. If I had attempted this concept one year earlier, I would not have understood it because I would not have been ready. I would not have succeeded. Now I did. I had faced my fears and lived to tell about it. There was no more dragon. What do you make of that?

Now that I have explored "false evidence appearing real" with you, allow me to turn to what is real.

Chapter 3

Anxiety and Depression

"A mistake in judgment isn't fatal,
but anxiety about judgment is."
—*Pauline Kael*

The Fall of My Life

I want to take a little time to talk about anxiety and depression. Some people argue that anxiety and depression are but secondary emotions to fear. Although I would not be inclined to disagree with this assessment on the surface, I still think it is distinct enough to merit its own attention. The simplest example I can think of is being anxious for Christmas when I already know what I am going to get. I am so excited to the point that I cannot sleep or fully concentrate on anything else. I am anxious to get this present and enjoy it. This is not a fear-based emotion. An estimated forty million people suffer from anxiety and depression, and forty-two billion dollars are spent every year on treatment for Anxiety and Depression. In a book about financial crisis, unemployment, and spiritual awakening, this subject deserves a hard look.

It seems like there are two ways to deal with anxiety and depression. I can choose to medicate so that I do not feel the feelings that make me anxious or depressed, or I can choose to change my feelings. I do not mean to minimize the devastating power of anxiety and depression on those who suffer from it; I was personally familiar with its strangling grip. I am only trying to break it down to its most granular components here.

I get anxious when I meet a new person, and it seems like the more I have at stake in this new encounter, the more anxious I get. An interview with a prospective employer is a very anxious moment. A first date is an anxious moment we can all relate to, and if it goes well, meeting the parents is an even more anxious occasion. Who among us was not anxious during our first speeches or debate classes? Going to a networking event was like anxiety on steroids for me. Then add to that the pressure that if these situations do not go well, it is depressing. It is very depressing to not do well in a job interview, and it is even worse to not get the job. It takes everything I have to keep looking, applying, and interviewing after a letdown like this. It is depressing when a first date goes wrong, and it's even worse when the dating starts out great but meeting the parents goes wrong; this tests the relationship to its very core.

At my first networking event, I thought I was going to throw up, pass out, or both, and I was physically, emotionally, and mentally spent when I returned home. Why do all these situations create such anxiety and depression for me? Because I want to be liked! How do I overcome this anxiety so that I can function in daily life? Guess what? Those who make you anxious want to be liked, too, and they are just as anxious in meeting you. They are also just as depressed when it does not go well.

Yes, I know, it's easier said than done. In her book *Hamster on the Wheel*, Helene Cho reveals a simple but very effective form of self-inquiry designed to question our thoughts, especially the stressful and judgmental ones.

There are four questions and what she calls the turnaround. These four questions are;

1) Is it true?
2) Are you absolutely sure it's true?
3) How do you react when you believe that thought?
4) Who would you be without this thought?

These four questions are a way of questioning our thoughts that are negative. The turnaround is the process of brainstorming, coming up with the exact opposite thoughts of what you believe. With these new thoughts, you can see if the turnarounds are also true or truer. Her book is full of delightful examples to teach you how to internalize the practice of this seemingly simple principal.

I recently caught the fever of a reality television show call *The Voice*. I do not define myself as a TV or reality show fan, so this is significant. The show starts out with four very prominent multimillion dollar international celebrities listening to unknown, wishful vocalists—but with the judges' backs turned to the singers so that they cannot see them and can only hear them. If they like what they hear, they turn their chair around, and that aspiring artist becomes a member of the celebrity's team to begin a contest to win a record contract. The twist is that if more than one celebrity turns around, the power shifts to the amateur, who gets to select which celebrity's team he or she wants to join. This point in the show is hysterical to me: people that we idolize get all twisted up while waiting to be picked by a "nobody." You can see their body language and their facial expressions, and you can hear their pleading to be picked. These celebrities are genuinely anxious. They want to be picked, they want to win, and they want to be liked. These are my favorite moments in the show because it is such a strong statement about how power, money, and fame cannot buy your personal security. Deep down, we are all the same: we all want to be liked.

When I was very young, I learned I was fast. I ran track through high school and into college. I also played football and wrestled in high school. Especially in track, every time I set into the blocks to start a new race, I began to sweat, became nauseous, and had the sudden urge to pee. I loved running. I loved the exhilaration of blasting out of the blocks. At the time, I never understood whether I was running away from something or after something; I simply knew I was not standing still, and this feeling was the only form of freedom my soul knew. I now know I was running from both the past and the future, making sure I was not stuck in the moment because I hated the feeling of the moment. I loved everything about running because it made me feel alive for ten seconds. I was anxious beyond human capability.

I was also a little of an oddball about competition. No-one, no-where, no how was bigger competition to me than myself. I perplexed my coach on the rare occasion that I lost a race but was happy because I had set a personal record—or more often, when I won a race but was deeply depressed that I had underperformed for my capabilities. All I wanted at the time was to be faster each time I strapped on those spikes and stepped on that track. The hundred meters is an addiction; it is not like team sports, like football. At nineteen years old, I ran the hundred meters in 10.64 seconds. For 10.64 seconds, I was out there all alone with nowhere to hide, and everyone could see me. In 10.64 seconds I demanded of my body what few people on this earth would even attempt. Those 10.64 seconds were the culmination of months and weeks and days and hours of gut-wrenching practice. I had 10.64 seconds to justify my existence on the track. I had the addiction.

I also experienced a lot of athletic injuries, starting with sprained ankles as early as fifth grade. Athletics was a very important part of my developmental years; it was more important to me than academics and extracurricular activities, and even more important than human interaction. When I was a senior in high school, I blew out a knee playing football. It was a very serious injury that sidelined me for most of the football season, and it decimated my final year of high school track. This was one of the most depressing moments in my life. I believed strongly that my speed was the only way I could afford to go to college and get out this town I had come to despise. The thought that neither would happen drove me into a deep depression and gave birth to dark, self-destructive thoughts and behavioral patterns. Something burned inside of me that pushed me, and as a result I learned the extreme polar opposites of anxiety and depression through victory and defeat, through excelling and being injured.

I did get well enough to run college track and excel at it for a short time, until the continued nursing of my knee caused a tear in my hamstring on the opposite leg, which was bearing the stress of me favoring the hurt knee when I ran. I was told at the time that I would never run again. This was another devastating moment in my life that very well could have destroyed me if not for the spiritual awaking I had experienced the year before. I was able to see my life differently: I saw a purpose now, not just an athletic event to win. I had redefined myself. I no longer ran because I needed to; I ran for the enjoyment and the interactions with my fellow competitors. But I still hated the start of each race.

Ten years later, I was married with children and working to support the family, but I had nursed my hamstring back to full recovery through the miracle of non-weight-bearing exercises like swimming and biking. I started running in master's track. I did very well for a short time until my knee injury reared its ugly head. Over the next twenty years, I had two arthroscopic surgeries that provided only temporary relief while I continued to experience the highs and lows of painfully competing in master's track through either less pain or more pain, but always pain. In the last five years, I wore an off loader brace all day and took it off only to practice or compete on the track. People must have thought I was insane, watching me show up at the track, take off my brace, pound out four four-hundred-meter or eight two-hundred-meter sprints, put my brace back on, and leave.

At fifty years old, my pain tolerance had reached dangerous levels, and I had exhausted all other alternatives. The meniscus in my knee was shot to the point that I could be walking on a smooth flat surface, and the knee would give out from atrophy. It was finally time to replace the knee—but Chase told me I had accepted the transition contract, so I could not have a surgery that was going to require time off work, or I would lose my retention bonus. The knee replacement would have to wait until I had a new job and was insurance eligible. Those three years were the most physically painful of all, and my physical activity was severely restricted. Even walking up stairs or the steep hills all over downtown Seattle was prohibitive. It was time for a knee replacement. I now maintain a theory that I suffered so many sports injuries because I was so possessed to keep pushing my body that I pushed it beyond its limits. I ignored the warning signs of pain and drove through it because I wanted to feel alive. I wanted somebody, anybody, to know that "I WAS HERE!"

In the fall of 2008, I attended a mandatory pre-knee replacement class at my doctor's hospital. In this class I learned about how reliant I would be on my arms to sit and raise from sitting during the knee replacement recovery process. This was problematic because I had been suffering from a progressively worsening tendinitis in my elbow that clearly would not bear my entire body weight without the assistance of my legs. I elected to have the elbow surgery first. While I was in recovery from the elbow surgery, WaMu collapsed, and I lost my job and my medical insurance. The knee replacement would have to wait until I was employed and insured once again.

As soon as I got my new job over two years later and became eligible for insurance, I negotiated with my boss for the surgery. However, by now a nagging pain in my toe on the opposite leg of my bad knee had turned into an inability to walk without pain as well. Again I knew that this toe could not bear the full weight of my body without the assistance of the other leg, so I opted to have a fusion done on my big toe before the knee surgery. The toe fusion required a longer, more painful recovery process than the knee replacement, and it required that I be non-weight-bearing on that leg for three months. They sent me home from the surgery with a knee cart to get around, but my knee on the opposite leg that was supposed to propel me around on the knee cart was my bad knee, and that rendered this contraption worthless.

The first week I was home, I was attempting to move from the couch to the knee cart. My bad knee buckled from the weight, and I landed flat on my back with my cast up in the air. This was the most helpless situation in which I had ever found myself. A loved one who was caring for me immediately arranged for a wheelchair, where I remained for the rest of that first month. The second month I graduated to crutches, but I still was not weight bearing, so I still relied on the bad knee to hobble around.

In the third month I migrated to a walking cast. This month was a gradual, progressive weaning off the crutches and on to the newly fused toe. During this month I was required to take a business trip. I consulted my physician, and he approved the trip. Even though I requested special assistance from the airline, I was appalled at the attitudes and treatment I received by them. On my flight out, I sat in cramped quarters with crutches and a cast up to my knee while six airline employees sat in the first row with all the leg room. Even though I was only one row behind them, they made sure not to make eye contact with me the entire flight. My boss traveled with me on the return flight. She suggested I practice a principle she calls "assume as." Even though the airline again refused to reassign me a seat in the front row, I sat there anyway. When the person with the assigned seat arrived, I explained I had the seat one row back but could not fit into it, and the person happily obliged me. I had taken on the belief that this seat was mine even though I did not possess physical evidence that it was and it became mine.

In this time of inactivity prior to and after my surgery, I gained weight for the first time in my life. I ultimately increased my weight by 30 percent. This was not my first major surgery; I already had four screws in my neck from a fusion, in addition to the four new screws in my foot from a fusion and perpetual scar tissue growth in my elbow despite arthroscopic surgery on it. But up to this point I had always maintained my high school weight. An estimated 70 percent of Americans are overweight, and for the first time in my life I joined this statistic, sharing in the sinking depression and self-destructive behaviors that accompany it.

All my thinking was getting me nowhere, so I sought the counsel of a nutritionist for guidance on what to do for an overweight, aging body in recovery from two major surgeries. In my case, all I needed to do was accept the reality that for a fifty-three-year-old, weight gain was a natural part of major surgeries. I joined far too many people in underestimating the toll that a major surgery had on an aging human body and the level of emotional, psychological, and physical effort it took to fully recover, including losing the weight gained from the surgery.

Just in case you haven't figured out how crazy I was, I elected to have the knee replacement one week after I got out of the cast from the toe fusion. The day of the surgery, they had me beginning physical therapy on the knee. Physical therapy turned out to be another life-changing event for me not because of the physical part—I was accustomed to recovering from athletic injuries—but because of the mental and emotional shift that transpired in my life as a result of this process. I had lived with knee pain for thirty-six years, since I was seventeen. As a result of sheer determination, I had developed some very self-destructive ways of getting around. The first thing that I learned about was the simple act of standing up from a chair, the sofa, or from bed. These were all very painful activities for me that most people probably took for granted. Because of the pain level associated with this one motion, I had learned to hold my breath and grimace with pain when I rose to my feet.

The first lesson of physical therapy was to exhale instead on inhaling when I performed this act. The act of holding my breath created all kinds of undue stress on the rest of my body. My muscles, diaphragm, and heart were being taxed by my insistence to find a way to function under the pain of the knee. By learning to exhale, I created an act of rising from my feet that lived in harmony with the rest of my body and became an effortless, daily occurrence. But the learning of this new behavior took painful hours of practice and frustration. I would spend an hour session with a physical therapist practicing nothing more than standing up from a chair the right way. "Exhale; use your knees, not your arms; use not your back, your knees," he would bark at me. "No, do it again—right this time." Then I would practice it at home and return the next week to demonstrate my progress. This took months.

This wasn't anything new. I had had the privilege of a professional trainer in collegiate athletics. We were all taught to exhale as we lifted weights or did crunches. I was taught in grade school to exhale as I exploded out of the blocks. This was not a new concept to absorb, but still I was incapable. I had trained my body to act one way for decades, and now I was telling it to do something different. This was not a simple task; it took work, determination, and endurance.

The second lesson of physical therapy that I learned was from my chiropractor. As he explained it to me, the act of limping for thirty-six years had completely realigned my back—in a bad way. Now that I could walk without a limp, my back needed to slowly and methodically be adjusted back into its natural alignment. In addition, the nearly complete deterioration of my meniscus, particularly on the inside of my knee, had caused me to become very bowlegged on just the one leg. When the surgery corrected this, it completely changed my gait when I walked. This was another long, slow path to normality for me. It is not a onetime solution. Adjustments were painful and liberating at the same time. Each adjustment brought me closer to my original self after a short period of the pain of difference, but the long, drawn-out process was a road of anxiety and depression, and many times I wondered whether I would ever get to the end of the road.

My struggle with weight further spiraled when, at an annual checkup less than a year after this final surgery, my doctor discovered a deep vein thrombosis category blood clot in my leg that sentenced me to another six months of inactivity, periodic monitoring, and a new lifetime habit of blood thinners. The size of the blood clot was so alarming that I spent the night in the emergency ward under critical surveillance, where I learned the practice of self-injecting warfarin into my stomach because pills did not enter rapidly enough into the blood stream, before they would release me from the hospital. Once I was able to return to the level of vigorous physical activity to which I was accustomed, I was able to start concentrating on my weight loss again. But the more I focused on it, the more it eluded me. The anxiety and depression led me to overeat on occasion, perpetuating the problem. As I slowly accepted that my weight-loss efforts were but a component of the natural course of the healing process, I began to lose weight. With the help of suggestions in eating habits from my nutritionist, a year and a half after the surgery and despite the clot, I have lost two-thirds of the weight I gained, and I continue on my path toward shedding the remaining one-third.

So what is the point of me including my physical therapy memoirs in this book? The parallelism is obvious to me. I had developed habits over a thirty-six-year period, and even though they were born out of the necessity to cope with a very difficult physical event, they were contributing to the further breakdown of my body. I see this as no different than the solutions I created to cope with a dysfunctional upbringing that ultimately contributed to my social retardation as an adult. In order to change the thinking and behaviors that were destroying me, I needed the assistance of a professional, and I needed a new way of seeing my condition, my rationalizations, and my alternatives. If this is not ping ponging between anxiety and depression, what is?

I found it necessary to reinvent myself, though I didn't understand what it was at the time. The process of reinventing myself began with redefining myself. Redefining myself began with nothing more than willingness. I differentiate willingness from commitment. In my experience, I can make a commitment to do something, but my will can still drag its feet, making it extremely difficult (if not impossible) to succeed in the commitment. My commitment to exercise more or eat less is quickly worn down by my unwillingness to make the necessary sacrifices. My complete and total willingness to change, on the other hand, makes my commitment seem easy. However, without action my willingness remains nothing more than just that. I like this trick question: Five frogs sat on a lily pad, and one made a commitment to jump off. How many frogs are left on the lily pad? The answer is five. The one frog only made a commitment—he didn't act on this commitment. I embarked on the willingness to revisit my life and see it through my "now" eyes instead of my "then" eyes. I sought to have a new experience with my life as I knew it. I became willing to set aside everything I thought I knew about myself, the world around me, and the invisible power at work in both. I made a commitment to have an open mind in the process.

The most important person in your entire life is your father. He has more power than anyone to influence you for good or for evil. What was your dad like? Did you have a good dad? When you hear the word *father*, does it conjure up amazing memories, bringing a smile to your face and joy in your heart? Or does it cause you to feel a sense of loss? Maybe you don't know your father. Maybe he abandoned you, betrayed you, died when you were young or disowned you. Maybe he has failed you or has become an enemy to you. Statistically, most men will grow up to me like their fathers, and most women will grow up to marry someone like their father.

Clearly the most significant impact on my life was my relationship with my father. Stay with me now—this is not Freudian "It's all my dad's fault" stuff. The emphasis is not on what my father did or didn't do; the focus is what I did with it and what am I going to do differently now by seeing it differently. My earliest preschool memories of my father are immensely joyous. Every evening, six days a week, my father returned home from work. It was always after six o'clock. My teenage and pre-teen siblings typically hid away in their rooms, and my mother was always in the kitchen preparing super for the family. My toy Boston terrier and I stood at the giant living room window, looked out to the street and the driveway, and anticipated his arrival. The terrier could hear his car before I could. His car stopped at one of the few stop signs in town and slowly rolled through the gravel that had not been compressed with the oil yet by passing traffic at the end of the block. As his car turned off the street and into the driveway, my heart would race with excitement. The car door would open, and when he stepped out of the car, closed the door, and walked up the sidewalk toward the house, I began jumping up and down. The front

The Fall of My Life

door to the house would open, the terrier would excitedly bark, I would run to my father, and he would grab me by the hands and twirl me around in the middle of the living room until Mom would step out of the kitchen to stop him and my siblings would come out of their rooms to see what all the racket was. Dad was home. No hug or kiss for his wife. No hello or "How was your day?" for my siblings. We just all sat down for supper. But I was on cloud nine.

On Sundays Dad did not work. In my younger years he would pack the family up in the station wagon, and we would take the preverbal Sunday drive. I enjoyed these trips. I always sat by myself in the furthest back seat that faced out the back of the car. I enjoyed watching the world as it went by, and we always saw something new as we went somewhere new. Somewhere along the way, in the not too distant future, I got too big to twirl, my siblings got to cool to hang out with the family, and these memories became just that, memories. The memories grew so faint that I began to wonder whether they were real or imaged. I grew up, and like an imaginary best friend, my dad disappeared with the harsh, cold realities of childhood and adolescence.

When I was twelve years old, my oldest brother was drafted into the Vietnam War and was not be seen for four years. My sister ran away from home and left the state, not to be seen again for ten years. My remaining brother went off to college two years later, and suddenly I was an only child in a house with two worn-out parents. I felt like I had become a nuisance and a burden. I felt like a mistake born to three siblings who were six, seven, and eight years old when I was born.

I went through this cyclical behavior throughout my middle school and high school years, to try and regain the intimate feeling I had with my dad as a preschooler. I acted out and learned about the confinement of juvenile detention. I excelled at sports, grew my long hair, and did too many drugs. I excelled at music, drank too much, I excelled at academics. I became sexually promiscuous. With each ebb and flow of my cries for help, I received only shallow, superficial, momentary recognition that did no more than propel me into the next phase. I remember far too many times the hollow feeling when I practiced and participated in an athletic, music, or academic event, and my dad was not there to witness it. His absenteeism evolved into a motivating factor for me to do well enough athletically to get out of his house and his town, and to go to college. Even though I had no idea what I wanted to do with college, I knew it would get me as far away from this feeling as I could possibly get. When I became of driving age, I disappeared for days at a time without notice, explanation, or remorse. After I graduated from high school, I packed all my belongings into my car and left for college. I did not say good-bye, and I had no intention of ever returning.

Halfway through my freshman year in college, I had a spiritual experience that changed everything about me and permanently altered the course of my life. I returned to my parents' home that summer and made my amends for everything I had put them through. I thanked them for everything they had done for me and told them that I loved them. They were either incapable or unwilling to reciprocate; all I got back from them was blank stares. But I had given myself a gift—the gift to see things differently. Even though this moment in time was a huge transformation for me, at the time it was but a small morsel of the journey ahead of me to free myself from how I learned to view myself and the world around me. I felt like I had had a banquet when in fact I had only unpeeled one layer of the onion. My dad died when I was forty-five years old. Even though I continued to practice love for him over those next twenty-six years, he died without ever giving me a hug or telling me, "I love you." I had zero comprehension as to what a significant impact his death had on me at the time. Having had a new experience with an open mind, I now know that my father's death impacted my life just as much as, if not more than, his life.

It was October 2003 when my brother called me to tell me he had taken Dad to the hospital because of dizziness and chest pains. Dad had not had a heart attack, but they had put a pacemaker in him. I made the five-hour drive to see for myself how he really was. Of course he would never tell me, but I had learned the art of nonverbal communication all too well from him. His body language, facial expressions, demeanor, and energy level were signs that he was feeling better than usual. I concluded the pacemaker was a success and returned home.

One week later I got another, now frantic, call from my brother; he told me that he had taken Dad back to the hospital, and they had transferred him to another hospital two hours away for specialized treatment because he was in critical condition. I rushed back to Oregon. We learned that the pacemaker was infected and that he now had a staph infection from it. They were trying to control the spread of the infection, but they needed to remove the infected pacemaker. However, the risk of a stroke at this point was probable. We gathered the family, and they lowered his medication enough that he could say his good-byes to us. I was sitting in a chair next to his bed when he gained consciousness enough to recognize us. The only words he spoke turned out to be his last words. He said with a crooked smile, "I guess this means I won't be going to the dance tonight." They took him into surgery to remove the pacemaker, and he suffered a major stroke that deemed him medically brain dead. I asked them to leave him on the ventilator that kept his heart beating until we could all say our final good-byes; as it turned out, I was the only one who wanted to.

I stood next to my father, held his hand, kissed him on the forehead, told him he was a good man and a good father, and said, "I love you." I held on to his hand while they removed his oxygen, and he breathed his last violent gasp. My father was dead. I did not cry. Neither the doctor nor the clergy could confirm or deny whether he could hear me. Even though I choose to believe he did, the point is that it really doesn't matter. I had not spoken those words for him—I had spoken them for me. I had unpeeled one more layer of the onion and had chosen to see my father in a different way. I was a father myself by now, and that helped. I realized that those evenings when he came home and twirled his preschooler around that he had just finished working a ten-hour day, and how exhausted it had to have been, yet he found the energy to twirl me before his super. I realized that all those times I wanted, needed him to be there to see me perform that he owned a business. He was supporting his family by running an old general store. He could not close the store to go see me, and he could not afford to hire someone else to run the store so that he could go see me. I realized he wanted to go see me as much as I wanted him to, and I realized that he hated himself for it. I understood that he was trying to keep a roof over my head. I now knew that he was doing the best he could with what he had.

I went home with my family, made all the funeral arrangements, and executed the estate without a will. I spent the next few months teaching my mother how to manage the finances, beginning with how to write a check and balance a check book. I rose to the occasion and got things done. I had no idea what was going on inside of me, and one day it all had to come out.

That same year, Luther Vandross released a song titled "Dance with My Father." This was his last recorded album; he won a Grammy for the album in 2004 and passed away in 2005. The song was a tribute to his father as he shared his childhood memories "before life removed all the innocence." He sang about his father "lifting him high" and "spinning him around." The song describes witnessing his mother's unbearable grief to the loss of her life partner, and his wish for one last chance to dance with his father again. The parallelism of this song gripped me and pulled at me, but it was still not enough to make me cry. It was not until the fall of 2008, just after the collapse of WaMu and the end of my marriage, that it all hit me. I sobbed like a baby for the loss of my father. I grieved for what never was and never would be. To this day I cannot tell this story of my father's death without at least choking up and getting misty eyed, just like I am right now as I type these words.

I know death all too well. I had lost both my grandfathers' when I was still in high school and both my grandmothers before the new century. I lost my sister at forty-eight years old, three years prior to my dad; a brother-in-law at only twenty-two years old a year later; a sister-in-law at forty-two years old four years later; my middle brother at fifty-six years old, four years ago; and my final brother at sixty-two years of last year. I have come to believe that all things happen for a reason and that good can come out of any bad. Each death has provided me the opportunity to experience each loved one differently, and it has strengthened my resolve to live each day to its fullest, to accept and appreciate my still-living loved ones for who they are, and to reinvent who I am, how I think, and what I do. Life is too damn short to do anything less.

    I grew up with my father's parents living four houses down from us in a little town of a hundred people. They were my babysitters when my parents went out, and my grandfather was my barber. I spent many summers vacationing with them. My grandfather taught me how to water ski before I entered grade school. He also taught me his secret to fishing, a sport at which he excelled. Because he was retired, he also had the time to watch me participate in sports. I recall that when I was in eighth grade, my grandfather came to a track meet where I not only won but set personal, school, and district records in four events. That day I felt like somebody recognized me and knew who I was. My grandfather was my father figure. He was not perfect; he had passed on to my dad his imperfections. But I felt like he at least knew I existed. When he died, it couldn't have been at a worse time for me. At the most confusing time in my life, the one person who knew who I was, was now gone.

My mother's parents were basically vagabonds. Every time we visited them, they were living somewhere different. At the time I thought this was cool and exciting, like an adventure that never ended. I got to spend vacations with them as well, doing nothing in particular and going nowhere notable, just like they lived their lives. It broke the monotony in my otherwise monotonous childhood. My mother's dad was her step dad, but I didn't know that until I was an adult; there was nothing that would have suggested it. He was the fun-and-games, lighthearted man that my father was not. He was the center of huge family gatherings around holidays, and that tradition died along with him. He was my first grandfather to die, and that event got me thinking for the first time in my life about what happens to someone when he or she dies. It was another burden I did not need in my life at the time.

My sister was one of the last, great classy ladies. I was able to rekindle our relationship after college when I moved to Seattle, where she had moved when I was thirteen. Even though her severed relationship with our mother haunted her to her grave, she carried herself with dignity and grace. I don't know how anyone could not like my sister. As it turned out, she was divorcing the man she ran away from home with ten years earlier at the same time that my first wife left me. We became best friends and even tried to set up each other on dates with our respective friends. She delighted me with a surprise birthday visit one year. Even though she lived a clean and healthy life, cancer took my sister at only forty-eight years old. I felt honored and privileged to be a part of her precious life, and to be one of the last ones to speak to her before she breathed her last.

My first brother died of a heart attack in a time of personal crisis for me, at the worst of my unemployment. We grew up at odds, had a tumultuous childhood, and avoided each other altogether as young adults. Somewhere in each of our maturation processes, we began to first tolerate and then actually enjoy each other's company. His was my hardest relationship to reconcile from the physical, mental, and emotional scars of our upbringing. He was the most like Dad of us three boys. He would talk about the weather and sports to no end, but I never heard him express a feeling. At fifty, he was diagnosed with cancer from a lifelong smoking habit. He appeared to have beaten it with chemotherapy and radiation, but at fifty-six he died of a heart attack from what I would consider the negative effects of his cancer treatment. The most difficult part of his death was watching my mother bury her second child, with her husband already passed.

My brother had just retired as a school teacher and track coach when he died. My mother, son, and older brother drove down to his memorial, which was held in the gymnasium of the only school at which he had worked during his thirty-five-year career. I was stunned when I walked into this gym to see a packed, standing-room-only crowd. Several fellow teachers, coaches, students, and athletes paid their respects in between tears. Even though he had taken our father's inability to communicate to the grave, he had found a way to touch the hearts and lives of hundreds of people across two generations. He had led a remarkable life; he had left a legacy. Today, in Track Town USA where Prefontaine and Nike were made household names, they also hold the annual Cantrall Classic in honor of my brother.

My oldest brother and last surviving sibling returned home to live with my parents when he was confined to an oxygen machine with only 15 percent lung capacity from a lifelong smoking habit. He was a high school standout and Vietnam veteran, but he lived his last decade in a physically miserable state of shortness of breath and pain. Although he was what some people would call an eccentric personality, he was by far the most open and honest of my family. The legacy he left to me was the challenge to maintain relationships. I saw through his death that the mass of friends he had accumulated was simply because he was a good friend to them.

I delivered the eulogy at his full-honors military funeral. It was an unusually clear day, the day after Memorial Day 2012 at Willamette National Cemetery in Portland, Oregon. As the graveside service came to its conclusion, I spied a huge hawk, it wings fully spread, gliding on the warm breeze overhead. As I pointed it out to the others and watched it effortlessly float, I could not help but wonder if this was the very spirit of my deceased brother demonstrating to me that I need not grieve his death, because now he was free, released from his decade-long interment of endless pain and suffering. As my mother and I drove the 120-mile, two-hour trip back to her home in my convertible with the evening sun warming us along the way, I saw a hawk (that one would think could not possible be the same hawk) a half dozen different times along the route, as if to continue to remind me that everything was all right, that he was free.

A particularly disturbing death to me was that of my sister-in-law. She was diagnosed with breast cancer at an unusually young age and endured the usual chemotherapy and radiation treatments. She had reached the ten-year anniversary of being in remission when a lower back pain developed in between her annual checkups; it turned out to be another form of cancer that had attacked so ferociously that it was inoperable by the time they detected it. She died within the year at forty-two years old. I never knew the women when she was not fighting cancer, yet she lived every day with gratitude, an infectious smile, and humor. I do not think I personally know a single person who has touched so many lives while she was dying. She left behind an equally remarkable teenage daughter that came to live in my home with my family until I moved out.

Perhaps the most tragic death I have been personally associated with was that of my last wife's younger brother. At only twenty-two years old, he had his life snuffed out fighting President Bush's war on terrorism five months after the 9/11 attacks. It was not only tragic that he died so young, but it was equally tragic that his entire family died emotionally along with him. He left parents, two sisters, and a brother behind with four nephews and three nieces, and they all crumbled under the sadness and despair of his loss. This once strong family nucleus remained weakened and vulnerable even six years later, when I left the home I had built together with my wife.

A final benefit of having a new experience with myself came in the form of a medical benefit, simply by learning—and I do emphasize learning—to accept life on life's terms. For years I had fought the misery of constant heartburn. I was on a prescription medication to fight the heartburn and its effects because not only was it making my daily life miserable, but when untreated, heartburn can literally eat you alive by destroying your esophagus. My personal experience is that this condition is oversold as being associated with what you eat. I ate many of the same food before, during, and after this condition. I my case it came and went with my level of anxiety and depression. After my new experience with my father, I saw the responsibilities in my life differently, and they lost their control over me. I refused to let the condition of the events and situations of this world control me, and I gained a self-realized freedom. As I took my life back, I quit having heartburn. I did not feel the symptoms of heartburn, and so I stopped taking the medication. That was five years ago. The ups and downs of what goes on in the world outside of my control still continue, but the way I choose to deal with them is within my control. I am healthier because of this empowerment. Anxiety and depression no longer control my life—I do.

Chapter 4

Reality

"We're not in Kansas anymore."
—*The Wizard of Oz*

A life lesson for me in relationship to reality is the principle of living in moment. There is a cute little saying that goes something like this:

> Yesterday is in the past
> and tomorrow is in the future,
> so the only day you really have is today,
> and that is why they call it the present.

Eckhart Tolle handles this subject perfectly in his book *Power of Now*.

My life lesson was about learning that this present moment is truly a gift. Now is the gift of life, and I did not even know it had been given to me. As it turns out, God always blesses me. Sometimes I know it. I had been living a life consumed by worrying about either the mistakes I had made in the past or the mistakes I was going to make in the future, and as a result I was missing out on the present. Worrying about the past was living in the past. Living in the past left me stuck in the past. Worrying about the future had me too focused on the future to notice the present. Admittedly, this can get tricky if I start trying to rationalize and justify my thinking, decisions, behaviors, and actions. After all, how am I supposed to learn from my mistakes if I don't examine the past? How am I to prudently prepare for my needs if I do not have plans for the future? I need to do both, but I need to do them in the moment. Reality is the present moment; it is all I ever really have. There is never a time when my life is not this moment.

I remember a church that I attended a long time ago. I really liked this church and the people who attended with me. I looked forward to Sunday all week long. As I slugged through the daily drudgeries at work and at home, my thoughts would often turn to how good it felt to be with my friends in church. But when Sunday morning came, I would sit in church, watch my clock, and count the minutes until it was over. I would say hello and good-bye, it would be over, and then there I was again. The minute it was over on Sunday afternoon, I was sitting in my pain and mourning its passing. This was insanity, yet I did it week after week for years because I could not—would not—live in the moment. Today when I am with friends whom I enjoy, I enjoy them, I pay attention to the inner feelings I experience, and I give them the dignity and respect that they deserve for choosing to invest the moments of their lives with me.

My life situation consists of certain things in the past that didn't go the way I wanted them to go. By continuing to resist what happened in the past, I still resist what is now. Hope is what keeps me going, but hope keeps me focused on the future, and this continued focus perpetuates my denial of the now and therefore of my happiness. The pain I create in the now is always non-acceptance of the moment, mental resistance in the form of judgment, or emotional negativity. The more I am able to accept now, the more pain-free I will be. When I fully accept my present reality, I accept what I have. When I fully accept what I have, I am grateful for what I have. When I am grateful for what I have, I am grateful for being. Gratitude for the present moment and fullness of life now is true prosperity.

Along with each divorce I experienced, my childhood insecurities over love and acceptance grew to monstrous proportions. As each relationship came and went, I was strangled by my past mistakes while I attempted to exist in even the tiniest of moments. My inability to foster and maintain a relationship in the past contributed to my pain and inability to function in relationships. As I stood idly by and watched one intimate relationship after another die on the vine, I became obsessed with the pain of the future and the pain of not having a moment in which to live. This pain prevented me from initiating potential new relationships that the universe presented to me. By recognizing my self-worth and the value I bring to a relationship because of the journey I have survived, instead of in spite of it, I empower myself to live joyously in casual, personal, professional, and intimate relationships. This inner joy allows me to live in the moment and be here now.

Fear is also linked to having my focus away from the now. When I am focused on the past, I struggle with my identity. When I focus on the future, I struggle with my fulfillment. I look at the present moment as either marred by something that has happened and shouldn't have, or as deficient because of something that has not happened but should have. If I do not like my "now," I have three choices: (1) remove myself from it, (2) change it, or (3) accept it completely. This is the message of the well-known serenity prayer:

> God, grant me the serenity to accept the things I cannot change, the courage to change the things I can, and the wisdom to know the difference.

This prayer now hangs on my wall at home. The first thing I needed to appreciate was that life would give me whatever experience was most helpful for me. When I truly understood this concept, I was able to understand that now was the experience I needed, because this was the experience I was having at this moment. Now I realize that my entire life journey ultimately consists of the step I am taking right now. There is always only this one step, and so I give it my full attention. This doesn't mean I don't know where I am going; it means this step is my focus, and the destination is secondary. What I encounter at my destination once I get there depends on the quality of this one step. If I cannot enjoy doing something, I can at least accept that it is what I have to do. Acceptance means that for now, this is what this situation or moment requires me to do, and so I do it willingly. Joy does not come from what I am doing; it flows into what I do with what I am doing. To accept what I have to do is to enjoy what I am doing already, instead of waiting for some change so that I can start enjoying what I do. I will enjoy any activity in which I am fully present, any activity that is not just a means to an end. Enthusiasm means there is deep enjoyment in what I do, plus the added element of a vision toward which I work. Even though I have a vision, what I am doing in the present moment needs to remain the focal point of my attention; otherwise I fall out of alignment with life's purpose for the moment and the vision.

Chip Kelly was the head football coach at the University of Oregon for four years. During his first year they went to in the Rose Bowl but lost. In his second year they lost the national championship by a field goal. His third year they missed out on a national championship bid with a defeat from USC by a field goal. In his final year they again just missed the national championship by a field goal loss to Stanford. Chip Kelly's motto was, "Win the Day." He repeatedly told reporters who relentlessly tried to trip him up that it does not matter if you won or lost the last game if you do not win this one. It does not matter that you are ranked first or second and positioned to play in the national championship if you do not win the game. Chip Kelly was not just teaching student athletes how to be the best at playing football; he was teaching young men to live in the moment. With his record, it is hard to argue with Chip Kelly (except that he needed to recruit a field goal kicker). It is no wonder that NFL team owners were knocking down his door to offer him a job.

As I began to practice the principals of the serenity prayer, I quickly became aware that the real trick is in the "having the wisdom to know the difference" part. The hard lessons for me do not exist in the black print in between the white spaces on the page; they exist in the white space in between the black print on the page. After all the print is read, life goes on in the grey area; this is where all the feeling and thinking takes place. Life is not black and white, it is grey. The wisdom to know the difference between what I can change and what I need to accept is not black and white; it is grey.

In my last marriage, I did not connect with my oldest step-son. Tried as I might, we were simply not on the same frequency. One of the most insane tricks I played on my own mind was telling myself that he was the source of my marriage problems. By doing so, I could convince myself that as soon as he graduated and left home, the marriage would be saved. He graduated and left home, and the marriage did not get better, yet when he came back, I still blamed the problems of the marriage on him. He was not the main source of our marriage problems—or even *a* source. He simply had his own demons to fight and was too preoccupied with his personal battles to contribute to a relationship with anyone else.

Our problem was mine, not his. Our problem was my inability to articulate and communicate what and how I felt about his behaviors without attacking him. I had been living in a future that never came, and as a result I denied myself, my wife, and her oldest son the benefit of me living in the present. Today, through the work that I have done, I have resolved this shortcoming, and it no longer prevents me from living in the moment. I am no longer paralyzed by the mistakes I made in the past, and I am no longer afraid that I will repeat my mistakes in the future.

I want to bring home three important principles here: clarity, intention, and attraction. My reality is knowing what I want, why I want it, and being able to tell your first grader in a way that he or she will understand me. In my personal experience, when it got painful enough I became motivated enough to explore these three concepts. Once I know what it is I want, I create my own reality with intention. Attraction is my radio waves of the same intentions out in the universe. There are countless books out there on these subjects; the ones that particularly spoke to me are listed in my appendix. Your reality is yours—learn it, own it, and protect it.

Clarity—how do I know the truth from a lie? How were Dorothy and her friends to know the Wizard of Oz was really just a man from Kansas behind a curtain? How was my sage to know the dragon at the entrance to the cave was only his imagination? Characters in movies often ask, "How do I know if she is the one for me?" What we are really asking is, "How do I know if I am thinking clearly? How do I know if what I am telling myself about my reality is false or true?" My conclusion: relationships!

It's funny how we keep coming back to this subject of relationships. Let's go back to the job search. Here I was networking my fanny off and being a resource to others. It slowly became obvious that I did not know what I wanted. How was it so obvious, you ask? Well, when someone asked me, "What do you want?" I stared at the floor and lost all my mojo, and the conversation quickly ended. That's how I knew I didn't know what I wanted. Back at the career center, "where everybody knows my name", my career coach and I had a new set of issues in hand. What did I want? Have you ever called someone and chatted a while, and then you say, "It was sure nice chatting with you, but what did you want?" and the person responds by saying, "You called me"? Well, that was me networking. Suffice to say that what I wanted in a job turned out to have a lot to do with what I wanted out of a relationship and what I wanted out of life. As it turned out, I needed to resolve those two questions first.

When I first met my sage and graduated past how to breathe again, he gave me an assignment: he asked me what I wanted in a relationship. Remember, up to this point, if you liked me then I loved you, so all I wanted was a warm body that liked me. I thought, *What do I want? Am I allowed to ask that, think about it, or dare to answer it?* So off I went to read and study, and I came back with a startlingly detailed list of what I wanted in a relationship, and I thought I was home free. My sage said that was great, and then he asked me a devastating follow-up question. "Would you want to marry you?" Ouch!

Before I say what I want out of a relationship, I have to be prepared to ask what I am willing to *give* to a relationship. Before I say what I want out of life, I have to be willing to ask what I am willing to give life. Before I say what I want out of a job, I have to be willing to ask what I am willing to give to that job. This is the natural order of the universe and how relationships are, making the world go around. If it is not give and take, then it is not by definition a relationship. Neither all the giving nor all the taking makes a relationship, a life, or a job.

I know that relationships can become a "crazy—maker", so let me point out what I learned. No one in this equation is perfect. We are all just doing the best we can with what we have at the time. What I want is not my demands or my ultimatums; what I want is what is important to me—some might say what is important to me are my boundaries where I end and where someone else starts. If I do not become willing to give what I want, then there is no relationship.

One would think that would be enough on this subject. But then I get the trifecta question: "How important is it to you?" Now I know what I want, and I am willing to give it as well, but how important is it to me? Say I want a blonde-haired, blue-eyed girlfriend. How important is it to me? What if I meet a green-eyed blonde that is everything else I was looking for? Wow! Now that is a dilemma, because I went through all this work to decide what I wanted. Oh, and it gets worse. What if I want sunshine out of life, and it gives me rain? What if I am offered a job that is everything I wanted, but it requires working for someone younger than me, and that is just not what I wanted? How important is the issue to me, especially if I have been out of work for over a year? Really, if someone offers me a fifty-dollar bill, am I going to say, "No, thank you. I wanted a twenty-dollar bill"? I don't think so, but we do silly things like this because we get it in our head that it's important.

So how did I answer this question? Very carefully, that's how. This is another thing you do not want to get wrong. It is not much different than the pros and cons lists we have all used to help us make an important decision. First we put all the pros and cons on each side of the paper, and then we prioritize them by how important they are. I could have only one pro and twelve cons, but if that one pro is my top priority, then it may be more important than all twelve of those cons.

It just so happened that at this time I was interviewing for a position with a very prestigious global firm, and as part of the screening process, they asked me to do a values exercise. It was at the time that I was doing this exercise that I connected the dots of how my values drove what was important to me.

My values are, in short, what is important to me, what I want to accomplish, and what I want to succeed at. My values should drive my thinking, my behavior, my actions, and my attitudes; if not, something is very wrong. Either my values are out of alignment, or my thinking, behavior, actions, and attitudes are off. My values are mine. Everyone is allowed to have their own values, and I am allowed to have my own. My values might and probably will change as I walk through the seasons of life but I must always realign my goals with them whenever they do.

After I completed my values exercise for the screening process and reviewed it with my prospective employer, I shared it with my sage. This is when I discovered he had boiled the frog alive (me being the frog). He had asked me in reverse order what I wanted and how important it was, backing me into the values question. In fact, it all works just the other way around. My values drive what is important to me, and what is important to me drives what I want. The blonde-haired, blue-eyed girlfriend is not a value. My value is that I take care of myself physically, and so I want someone in my life that does the same. I had only conjured up an assumption, perhaps based on some personal or observed experience, that blonde-haired, blue-eyed girls share the value of taking care of themselves physically, but that is not reality. After all, we all "know" that "blondes have more fun" if we grew up with a TV. This value drives the fact that this is important to me, and that importance drives the fact that this is what I want. She may be blonde or she may be black, and she may have blue eyes or they might be brown, but it is important that she takes good care of herself because that is a core value to me.

The stereotypical American dream is the house with the white picket fence. Now, if I make this my want, I am going to have a problem because there just aren't houses with white picket fences to be found anymore unless I build my own. But how important is it to me? Does the fence really have to be white or picketed, if the house and yard are everything else I ever dreamed of? What is my core value here? It is to be able to buy and own real estate that I can put up a sign and call home. The type and color of the fence are not I what I want—my place in the world is what I really want.

I have applied for jobs at companies in the past that used Myers Briggs type indicators as part of their screening process. They are after the same understanding: what are my default behaviors? They know that those behaviors are tied to my values, and they want to know if my values are aligned with the company's values. You can also make a company apply for your values. For instance, through this exercise one of the things I found to be important to me is how a company treats its employees. There it is again—that idea of relationships. What a surprise that this would turn up as one of my core values. One thing I wanted in a new job was a company that treated its employees well.

Now that I have created my own reality and have found clarity around that reality, here comes the "woo-woo" part—the law of attraction and the power of intention. I hope I do not lose you here; please hear me out. This is not your father's religion, and this is not "positive thinking" or "new age philosophy." In fact, I do not want to call it anything or try to put it into any box because it is older than dirt itself. It is the higher self, the true self. I found this to be quite practical in my life, and I have to say that of all the books out there on this subject, Wayne Dyer's are the best for me personally.

I am a visual person, and so I understand this concept as radio waves. We all walk around with little transmitters and receivers. Each of us is on our own frequency. The people that happen to be on the same frequency transmit and receive each-others signals. Have you ever tried to communicate with someone who just seemed to be on a different frequency? Well they were, at least from you that is, but not from others. And so it is with our millions of everyday thoughts. We attract what we think, and what we think may not be what we intended.

Let's use my previous example. My thoughts are of the American dream with a blue-eyed blonde girl in a house with a white picket fence. But every blonde I meet is dumb, and every house with a white picket fence is old and run down. I did not attract what I wanted because my thoughts are not my true intention. What I need to understand is that my core values are to be in a relationship with someone who takes care of herself, and to own a home. Then I can align my thoughts with that intention and attract it. Now, that isn't so "woo-woo," is it?

At this point I had processed a life lesson and was ready to go back to the career center to apply it to my career coach's question: what did I want in a job? I had just survived the exercise of what I want in a relationship; I was now ready to apply what I learned to the job (and later on to life). Now I can go out networking, and when people ask me what I am looking for, I know what I want, why I want it, and I can tell your first grader in a way he or she will understand me. There are those of you who knew me at this point in time, and I will bet that you can still recite my answer even to this day, because it was simple, short, and spoken with power and deep conviction. This is why. This is the process I went through to get to that point.

But now that I am in touch with my values, wants, and intentions, how do I attract what I want into my life? Do I sit on the floor cross-legged, chanting and attracting everything I want? Do I take out an advertisement on the billboard at Times Square and announce it to the world? Do I post it on Facebook? Where is the balance? I followed three simple steps.

1) Dream—no, dream big
2) Get out of the house
3) Leave no stone unturned

Let's break this down. First, don't just dream, but dream big and visualize. This is how it worked for me. When I was asked what I wanted in my next job, I closed my eyes and saw myself walking into the office on my first day. I saw what I was wearing and what everyone else was wearing. I saw how people reacted to my arrival. I saw whether they were friendly or scurried away. I saw what my work space looked like. I saw whether it was a corner office or a cubicle. I saw the type of work I was doing. You get the point—visualize it. Do you like what you see? If your vision is not working for you, then get a new one. Go back to go, do not collect $200 dollars. Start over with your core values.

If a Blue-eyed, blonde girl, a house with a white picket fence, sky diving, or swimming the English Channel are things that are of your core values, attract them by visualizing what it would be like to have them as if you already do. I am going to cheat here because it is too irresistible, and I am a rule breaker. I am going to let you in on a piece of the end of the story. My boss today lives by the mantra "Assume as if," and it is amazing what she attracts into her life by doing so. I admire and respect many things about her, but this is at the top of the list. And by the way, I attracted this boss into my life, so between the two of us, watch out!

Ok, so now I have shown you that my boss and I "dream big" and visualize "as if." Now it is time to get out of the house. I learned my dreams were not going to come true while sitting cross-legged on the floor and chanting. It doesn't matter how much I visualize; the only way to make dreams come true is to put legs on them. For the job seekers out there, I share a very painful realization. I had to get out from behind my computer and go meet someone, anyone, for coffee. I just had to get out the house. Why? Because getting out of the house gets me out of my head, and my head is a neighborhood in which I should not be alone. My head is where the dragon and wizard live, where there are lies and more lies that cripple me and can destroy me.

I have been there and have witnessed this. Perfectly capable, highly qualified, and otherwise likable people are pounded into the ground, hiding behind the computer, applying for job after job online, and getting nowhere. How painful did it have to get before I was willing to try something different? How scary could a cup of coffee be? I started with someone I knew who wasn't so scary to me. See for yourself what it will do for you. I cannot emphasize this point enough: get out of the house before it is too late. Get out now! Pretend the house is on fire or something, but whatever you do get out!

What I found was that when I got out of the house, it was like a breath of fresh air. The dragon was just in my imagination, and the wizard was just a plump old man from Kansas. No one bit my head off, told me I was stupid, or a myriad of other visions I had conjured up in my head. People are generally good, nice, and willing to help. I saw a whole different side of life, and it energized me to want more, so I did it again. When I got out of the house, I got better. I started using the career center (where the career coaches met with job seekers) as my office. I got up every morning, got dressed, and went to the office just like I had a job. I conducted my job search as if it *was* my job, because, guess what, the reality was, that it was my job and my only job was to get a job. Anyone who was in this position will say that the hardest job they ever had was looking for a job.

This principle does not apply to only job seekers. Somewhere along the line, Americans stopped socializing. Television and the Internet provide a virtual reality to the point that we do not know what reality is. I am here to shatter a paradigm: reality TV is not reality. If I want to meet the blue-eyed, blonde-haired girls, I need to get off the dating site with criteria set to blue-eyed, blonde-haired girls and go to the blue-eyed, blonde haired girl's convention. Oops, girls only? Oh well. If I crash it, I am bound to get noticed by a blue-eyed, blonde-haired girl.

Okay, I am making light of a very serious, psychological phobia, but you get my point, right? If I want to meet people that I will enjoy, I need to go do something that I enjoy. If I go skydiving, then lo and behold, I may meet a green-eyed blonde girl that loves to skydive and turns out to be my soul mate. Once I know what my core values are and what I want, I need to go out and get it. The universe will hear my radio signals and will return to me all the other radio signals on my frequency; it can't not do this. It is the physical law of the universe. It really is that simple, that true. When I put loving thoughts and behavior into the universe, I plant seeds of self-worth. When I put unloving thoughts and behavior into the universe, I destroy seeds of self-worth. Identification with an unhappy and deeply fearful self is ultimately a fiction of the mind.

I am a banker, and this makes sense to me because I do not see it any different than deposits and withdraws on an account. If I deposit into my account, it grows. If I withdraw from my account, it shrinks. It is okay to withdraw when you need to, but if you withdraw more than you deposit—in other words, you take more than you give—then you are going to get that right back from the universe in the form of an overdraft notice with a hefty fine attached. And if you do not make good on the overdraft, your account will be closed and you will not be able to go anywhere else or open a new account until you do.

Another way to exercise self-worth is through affirmations. A simple Google search tells us that our brain processes at least an astronomical 70,000 thoughts per day and up to 150,000. That is at least 2,916 per hour, or 48 per minute, or almost one per second. Google also references several Clinical Studies that claim 80 to 90 percent of those thoughts are negative. Susan Jeffers coins these negative thoughts "the chatterbox." I have heard others call it "the committee" because, as with most committees, there are a lot of voices speaking at the same time, and nothing gets done. Affirmations are a simple way to quiet down the chatterbox. Especially at first, I do not have to believe my affirmations for them to work; I simply need to replace the negative self-talk with positive self-talk. Susan Jeffers offers numerous exercises to accomplish this in her book *Dare to Connect*. The primary point for me was to get to a place where no matter how someone else responds to me, I know that I am a worth-while person. I can come from a place of seeing others as myself, wanting to be liked and I can extend acts of caring. Acts of caring are what makes life worth living.

Now I have a dream that I have visualized, and I am out of the house. Maybe I should be a little more specific with what I am supposed to do out here. OK here it is. "Leave no stone unturned." I remember going for a walk with my then toddler son on a fall day. I knew I should not be in a hurry, or else both of us would be frustrated. His curiosity was immense, and he wanted to stop to see and touch everything. His innocence wanted to leave no stone unturned because he didn't want to miss anything—and I mean anything. Now that I think about it, at twenty-six years old, he is still this way.

This is what I am talking about. I have to put aside all my preconceived notions and assume nothing. I have to get out there like my toddler son, exploring everything for the very first time. I am here to tell you, "You do not know what you do not know." In the job search you do not know who knows who. I can provide you pages of examples where I was surprised or disappointed that things did not turn out the way I thought they would, but I would have never known if I had not gotten out there and tried. For instance, two big, mistaken assumptions made in the job search are "The secretary doesn't know anything" and "You can't talk to the big dog." I am here to tell you the secretary knows everything, and I have talked to the big dog. Why do these misperceptions exist? Because people think they know, but they really don't. I did not assume either to be true, and I found out neither was. Nothing is as it appears.

I have been in a restaurant, noticed a man or a woman, and thought to myself, *Oh wow, they really have it together. They are so well dressed, and they are the center of attention and are so confident.* What a load of crap. I don't know that person from Adam or Eve. Maybe she just checked her only son into rehab. Maybe his wife is at home with a breast cancer diagnosis that she hasn't told him about yet. Maybe her father has Alzheimer's. Maybe he is going to lose his job tomorrow. In fact, the odds of any one of these events being true are far more likely than my passing assumption based on dress and mannerism.

You do not know what you do not know. Do I think the beggar on the corner is stupid and lazy? Do I think that Bill Gates never disagrees with his wife, Melinda, over money? Would I love to have a movie star, professional athlete, or rock star life? Things are never as they appear. I had to stop assuming everything, stop passing judgments (positive or negative), and take on the innocence and curiosity of my toddler son, during a walk on a fall day. When I did, a whole new world opened up for me, just like it did for my son. It was a world full of wonderful surprises that make my heart sing and my toes tingle. It just makes you want to dance, doesn't it?

Another taste of reality applies to the over-forty job seeker, and I assure you this is going to go exactly the opposite direction of your first instinct, so listen up. The financial crisis of 2008 displaced millions of workers over forty (or in my case, over fifty). But the title of Robin Ryan's book is *Over 40 and You're Hired*, so she wins. If you are what she coins the "mature worker," this book is a must. Robin interviewed numerous HR leaders and top executives. They insisted that they do value the experience and skills of the mature candidate, but they clarified that the mature candidates do not know how to market themselves. Do you hear that? I had to drop all my old, preconceived conspiracy theories about age discrimination and pick up Robin's book. She walks through how to be a successful, mature job seeker.

Fear, Anxiety and Depression distort Reality. By understanding and knowing my Values, what is important to me and what I want I create my own reality. Regardless of what all the physical evidence indicates I am the master of my own destiny. I do not have to take whatever live gives me. I get to decide what kind of life I have. No one else has that power over me. It is mine and mine alone.

Chapter 5

Mechanics

"We're gonna need a bigger boat."

—*Jaws*

The Fall of My Life

I am going to devote this chapter primarily to my job search, but I will try to relate it to the other aspects of my life because they are so intertwined. Even though up to this point I have covered a lot of the internal work I did in my job search, the reality is that there are still a lot of mechanics involved in the job search. There are countless resources available on the how-to of the job search. I would not be doing justice to my journey if I did not include this chapter on these mechanical aspects of my job search and what worked for me. Just as the internal work would have been of no value to me in my job search if not for the mechanics, the mechanics would have been of no value to me if not for the internal work I did.

Let me go back to my meeting in the career center with my career coach, when I sheepishly surrendered and asked, "How do I network?" One of the mechanical steps to this was using LinkedIn. As I said before, at that time I had two friends, and one was my dog. So what was I to do? First I threw a tantrum about it, and then I felt sorry for myself. Then I looked up, looked around and suddenly I had an idea. I started by asking the twelve people in my department at WaMu to join my network on LinkedIn; after all, they were all looking for work, too. I could do that. Much to my surprise (honestly, I was surprised), they all accepted. And then an extraordinary thing happened. I noticed they had connected to other people as well. They had one leg up on me—they had already been doing this networking thing. But being the sharp mind that I am, I began to notice a trend. The other people they were connected to were people I also knew. So I cleverly deduced that I could ask these people to join my network as well. So I did. I could do that. And much to my surprise, (yes, honestly, I was still surprised), they accepted my invitation as well. I hope I have demonstrated the power of how LinkedIn works by now. Mechanically, LinkedIn quickly became my strongest job-search tool. When I realized its power, I stopped applying for jobs online completely. Yes, that is right. The day came when I never applied for a single job on-line again.

Here I am going to cheat again, because it is just so darned fun. I am a manager now, and I have hired thirteen people in the last year. I have not recruited for a single job yet. I have hired all thirteen employees by word of mouth and based on personal referrals. My boss frequently compliments me by reminding me I have the "A" team. It was a pivotal point in my job search when I came to this reality. Actually, two events transpired almost simultaneously. The first was that my career coach (there she is again) recommended Robin Ryan's *Over 40 and You're Hired* (the follow-up to *60 Seconds and You're Hired*). There is one page in this book that changed my life: page 54. My career coach calls that page "a day in the life of a hiring manager." In short, it talks about how a hiring manager needs to replace an employee who has just resigned and is willing to go to any lengths to avoid having to use the long, drawn-out HR process. The hiring manager prefers a referral from a trusted source.

At the same time, I had an informational interview with a hiring manager at a very prestigious global firm based in Seattle. He explained to me that at the time, for every opening he posted, he received four hundred applications. Because of the high response, HR would only give him internal applicants' resumes; there were usually fifty or those, and he would have his own stack of personnel referrals, usually another fifty. Now he had one hundred resumes, all from highly qualified internal candidates and personal referrals sitting on this desk. How did he decide who to hire? He decided by whom he knew and trusted the most. If I know Sam and he referred Sally, but I *really* know and trust Jane and she referred Jim, then Jim is my man.

By the time I started attending networking events, I had a couple hundred connections just from linking in with colleagues with whom I had worked. Remember, when I attended a networking event, I tried to be of service, and LinkedIn turned out to be an invaluable tool for me. When I met people at a networking event, I kept it concise but would conclude our chat by asking for a business card and inviting them to join me on LinkedIn to see whom I was connected to that they might want to meet. After I had been of service to them, they practically begged to help me. I would invite them to coffee and hit them with my elevator speech. When I landed my job less than a year after I had started building my LinkedIn network, I had over nine hundred connections that I knew personally. Today I have attracted over 1,200 connections from people who want to know Bob, and I remain open to coffee for anyone who asks me.

By contrast, I'd like to pause here and attempt to relate the process I went through to components of my personal life. I have already shared the power of LinkedIn in the job search, but there are people who add thousands of connections to their LinkedIn profiles just so that they can say they did it. They think it makes them look influential, but remember that nothing is as it appears. They do not necessarily know the people to whom they connect; they have an electronic connection, but they do not have an actual relationship connection. If I asked them to introduce me to their LinkedIn connections, they would not be able to. I think this is pointless; it is not what LinkedIn was designed to do.

Facebook is clearly the predominate social networking site out there today. Internet socializing seems like a contradiction in terms to me. If it connects people, then God bless it. But I want to challenge this thinking for a moment. Facebook can create the same trap. For example, if I add to my friends list a cheerleader I went to high school with thirty-five years ago, I did not truly connect with her. I do not currently know anything about this person. We share pictures of kids, tell each other where we work, and where we went on vacation, and we imagine we are connected. She is, in my mind, still the person I knew in high school, frozen in time, but I don't really know who she is or what she is like today. If I want to really connect with her, I need to go have a cup of coffee with her, go over to her house, and meet her husband, kids, dog, and goldfish. Facebook can be an awesome way to easily reconnect, but do not be fooled—it is only an electronic connection until people build or reestablish an actual, personal relationship.

In addition, I have seen too much evidence that there are few reputable dating sites that are not paying people to lure others into memberships with promises and lies. For the few that may be reputable, I remain puzzled as to why people present themselves to be someone they are not, when sooner or later they are going to be found out. If I want a relationship with someone who likes to bowl, wouldn't it be simpler to get out from behind the Internet, go down to the bowling alley, and join a bowling league? I doubt that there is anyone there who is trying to pick up bowling people but actually hates bowling. If I am looking for a soul mate to dance with, then I need to sign up for a dance class. Odds are someone else has had the same idea.

Another amazing mechanical tool I utilized for my job search was a target list of companies. Let's go back to the career center, when my career coach asked me what I wanted. Mechanically, it was a very specific exercise. My career coach provided a template. In the first column I wrote what I wanted in very specific terms. I included location, private or public or not-for-profit, age, industry, and product, number of employees, values (there that is again), culture, structure, and leadership. I wrote whatever I deemed to be in alignment with my core values and I decided I wanted in a job. To do this, I needed to visualize my dream job. I listed the names of the companies that fit those criteria across the top row.

Herein lies "the shift." There is no other way to describe it. It is that point in time when I stopped applying for jobs and started interviewing companies to learn which ones met *my* criteria, which ones might house my dream job. This was my secret. It was a pivotal point not just in my job search but in my life. This was what changed everything for me. This was when I understood I did not have to take what life was giving me—I could go after life and take what I wanted. And this was how I did it. I would not have been capable of this a year earlier, but now, after I had done all the other work, I was ready.

We are all familiar with the television series "friends" and the lyrics in their theme song; ". . . you feel like you're

The Fall of My Life

always stuck in second gear . . .". This is the moment you shift out of that low grinding gear that will not let you gain any momentum into high gear. This is the mentality that shifts the power of the job search from the company to the employee. This is the shift that employs all the forces of the universe in your behalf.

To complete this exercise, I again turned to LinkedIn, which has tremendous search capabilities. I have shown many people how to use this tool because it is invaluable. I used the filters and searched for companies that met my demographic criteria. Much to my surprise, I found one hundred companies that fit the profile of my dream job on the surface. By this time I had accumulated a few hundred connections, many of them former WaMu peers; now, they had begun landing jobs across all industries and demographics of companies, and they had friends and family even more widely spread.

This was where LinkedIn was truly powerful. For all one hundred companies that were on my dream job list, I could find at least one person who knew at least one person in that company, and many times it was more than one person. I contacted the people I knew and told them what I was doing, mentioning that they knew someone at one of my target companies that I wanted to talk to. Then I asked them to introduce me on LinkedIn. Everyone (yes, everyone, with no exception) was willing to do this for me.

Once introduced, I asked these people to have coffee with me so that I could talk to them about their company.

I have a dear friend who had been unemployed longer than I. He had a colleague he'd worked with years ago, but he was afraid to ask him to connect on LinkedIn even though he was quite sure this person could provide employment. He questioned whether they were on good terms and was afraid this person did not like him. Even though I tried to help him understand that he had nothing to lose and that the worst the colleague could do was not answer, he was still stuck. My friend finally paid a professional, who also told him to send the invitation to connect, and he finally did. He was employed one week later. Oh, the barriers we can create in our own minds!

Listen up, freshman! I never-but-never asked for a job or handed out a resume. I was there to build a relationship. I was there to listen to others talk about themselves and about their companies. And I am here to say that everybody likes to do both. All I did was ask questions, sit back, listen and take notes. I was learning whether each company fit my criteria. I showed up on time professionally dressed, stuck to my predetermined agenda, honored our allocated time commitment, and thanked the person for his or her time. That was it. If in the course of our chat the person I was interviewing felt a connection with me and was so inclined to ask me how they could help me, I was prepared to be professional and concise with my reply. Sometimes people did ask, and sometimes they didn't ask until I provided my follow-up thank-you e-mail.

I kept my list of one hundred company's current, and I brought it with me to every informational interview. Under each company name, I listed the individual with whom I had spoken, who had facilitated our introduction, and the names of those to whom I still wanted to speak. In one informational interview, I was stopped cold in my tracks ten minutes into my requested half hour; the woman asked straight up to whom I wanted to talk. I showed her my list of companies with individuals' names. She whipped out her Blackberry, and before I could blink I had three new appointments that she'd scheduled for me. That is the power of knowing what I want and making it so clear that a first grader can understand it.

Regarding the follow-up, I always circled back to let the person who had introduced me to my new contact know that we had followed through and met, and how the contact had specifically been helpful to me. I would let them know how I liked it in the same way I'd review a recommendation for a restaurant or a movie. This is just plain common sense and good etiquette, but it is a critical step that people often overlook. This is a relationship, not a means to an end. Treat it like a relationship. To this day I have distaste if someone asks me to connect them with a contact of mine and then never lets me know how it went—or worse, never bothers to follow up to contact the person after I introduce them. I am going to be less willing if not unwilling to help this person out a second time.

I landed several interviews through this process, but more important, I was able to eliminate companies from my target list as I learned from insiders that these companies were not a match for my criteria as my dream job. Does this sound like a familiar theme? I have to admit here and now this is not exactly how I ultimately landed my current job, but I will explain how this strategy and process is what got me in front of the person who ultimately created my dream job for me. Furthermore, this is work I would do all over again in a heartbeat, regardless of the outcome. There was a moment when I wondered if I could make a living at networking. Never before this point would I have thought I would consider it fun and fulfilling.

Let me clarify that I did not buy a magic bean, and I was not a gifted interviewee. The very first informational interview I conducted was a disaster, and it was only over the phone. I was not prepared, I was not practiced, and I was not confident. It was short, and it was painful for both of us. But I took the next indicated step and sought help. I went back to the career center—I would think they would be sick of seeing me drag my sorry self in there by now. They were offering video-taped mock interview sessions with professional feedback. How could I not take advantage of this? Let me say that many people did not because they could not overcome their fear of what they would see or be told. It was an invaluable experience, and I believe that those who could not participate sold themselves short—their fears held them back. I was able to see myself as the interviewer saw me. In fact, she was so good at this that she had me wanting to work for this fictitious company she created on the fly while I asked her my list of questions.

I got both positive and constructive feedback. I was able to hear myself, and I received remarkable advice on how to improve my technique when conducting informational interviews. I was pleased to receive positive feedback that I interviewed with "quiet confidence," I spoke with professional polish, and portrayed confidence in myself and my capabilities. I was challenged to be more personable, especially during the initial ice-breaking portion of the interview. Specifically, I was advised to make a personal connection before I got down to business, as a way of setting the tone for the rest of the interview.

I took what I learned and scheduled my next informational meeting. It went a little better but was still not what I had envisioned, so I discussed what I had learned and what I had experienced with my career coach, making more adjustments. I scheduled another interview, and it got better. I reviewed and tweaked some more. This cycle continued until I was getting what I wanted out of these interviews. I knew what I wanted, and I created my own reality. Now I was on a roll.

I hope everyone understands the significance of this exercise. That it was interviewing I was concentrating on at this point in the process is quite irrelevant. My point is that I was given an opportunity to learn and grow. I pushed through my fears, and I did it. As I got better at it, it got easier to do until I finally saw it materialize into what I set out for it to be. I was not special in any way; I was simply willing to put in the work because I was desperate to get out of the darkness in which I was living.

I mentioned that if and when someone asked me how they could help me, I was prepared. There is a mechanical aspect to this as well: it is a tool that my career coach picked up from Duncan Mathison. Mathison is the author of *How to Unlock the Hidden Job Market*. He calls it a "targeted opportunity profile," or TOP. The key element to the profile is that unlike the resume (which talks about where I have been), the TOP illuminates where I want to go (another familiar theme). My profile consists of what differentiates me, what I will do, which key competencies I will use, what I will be called, to whom I will report, when I will add value, and where I will fit in.

In addition to the practical usefulness of the profile, the process of creating it was worth the soul-searching it required. This exercise forced me get away from the drudgery of trying to customize each resume to convince each employer that I could perform in the role they wished to fill. It forced me to think about what I wanted in a job and how I needed to position myself to get it. It forced me to create a clear vision of my dream job so that anyone who read this document would understand how to assist me. The TOP was a way to create my own reality, and it did.

The litmus test of the targeted opportunity profile is whether my spouse or teenager understands it. Think about it. Put down this book right now and ask your loved ones if they can describe in detail what you do for a living, let alone what you *want* to do. Can they explain it to another relative or friend? You may be surprised and dismayed. With a well-written TOP, they will know. Once I had the TOP, I never again handed out a single resume, and I never asked for help in getting or applying for a job opening. I handed out the professional profile, and I asked to be introduced to the people on my target list to whom I could talk about my dream job.

A dear friend whom I met networking was in Costco one day, pawing through a messy pile of clothes and looking for her size. A man walked up to her and commented what a mess it was. As a professional merchandiser, she knew this business, and she let him know it. She commented that there was definitely a better way to do this. He introduced himself as a merchandizing executive at Costco. He explained that he was looking for a strong businesswoman, and she had an interview the following week. This is another example of the benefits of knowing what she wanted and making it so clear that her first grader could understand it. She was very disappointed to not get this job, but she learned firsthand a valuable lesson in being prepared and articulate. She nearly lost her home while she accepted two new jobs that did not work out, but she pushed herself past her self-defined limits and landed her dream job. It was a privilege to participate in her journey.

During the year that I actively utilized the resources of the career center, I heard countless stories from job seekers who were naturals at developing networks, contacts, and referrals through the barber, the concierge, people on the bus, train or carpool, friends at church, fellow soccer mom's. The list goes on and I was always listened to these stories in wonder and thought, *How can I ever do this?* I was not so different than anyone else. To steal the motto from Nike, I just did it.

My last piece of mechanical work was the most challenging for me, and it indicates why I am not in sales. I was just trying it on when I landed a job, and so I did not get to feel comfortable with it and conquer it. Anthony Paenello wrote a book titled *Selling to VITO (the Very Important Top Officer)*. The idea in a nutshell was to find the top dog and convince him he needs me. I was excited about following the formula, so I wrote the top dog at one of my targeted companies and called to follow up a few days later. This felt like stepping off a cliff in the pitch dark, even after all the other work I had done. I was so full of fear that when VITO answered the phone I choked and stumbled all over my words. He hung up on me. There, I am human.

I still believe strongly in this concept and strategy, and for those who are in sales, I highly recommend it. I did not push forward with it myself because I landed my dream job. I know that had I not found the job I now hold, I would have had to face my fears and become comfortable with this strategy. I allowed my fears to creep back in simply because I was talking to the top dog, and I let that intimidate me. I reverted to fear. Fear of not being liked. Fear of looking stupid to a "superior" being. I was emitting that particular radio wave, so that was the reality I created. I sounded stupid, and he hung up on me because he did not like me.

The final mechanical theme I'd like to share is gratitude. Even practicing gratitude alone will change your life. If a person is feeling sorry for himself because of his lot in life, and he begins to focus on what he does have to be thankful for, it will turn his life around. This is more than just the "glass half full" theory. Gratitude is about understanding what we *do* have and being thankful for it. It is a way to reclaim clarity and reality. It may be hard to do at first, but it gets easier with practice.

While I was losing everything material and financial in my world, the one thing that I was able to do while I was learning my many other lessons was to practice an "attitude of gratitude." Every day I reminded myself of what I had to be thankful for, and I knew there were people far worse off in the world than me. One of the practical ways I do this is by sponsoring a little girl in El Salvador, which is the poorest country on our continent. I have supported this girl for ten years now. My sponsorship has allowed her to go to school, and now she wants to be a school teacher. When I was at my bottom, I knew one thing for certain: I would go without before I stopped sponsoring this little girl, because no matter how bad things got for me, I was far better off than she could imagine herself to be. Perspective and gratitude saved me from despair and depression.

The mechanics are the nuts and bolts that actually put the whole thing together. If I have all the nuts and bolts, but I do not have the rest of the parts or the instruction manual, then I cannot put it all together. If I have the rest of the parts and the instructional manual, I still have nothing without the nuts and bolts. Thus it was for my job search. I needed to know and understand the how, but without the gut-wrenching, soul-searching internal work, the how would have been of no use. Even after I had found the instruction manual for my life, I would not have been able to find another job with a thorough understanding of the how. Ask any mechanic how protective they are of their tools; without them, their very livelihood is threatened.

Chapter 6

Relationships

"Everybody's always talkin' about love. Yuk!"
—*Sesame Street*

By now, it should not be surprising that this book would cycle back to a chapter dedicated solely to relationships. Needless to say, my life lesson these past four years is that relationships are all that really matter. Without relationships, nothing else works. With every corner that I came to, every page that I turned, the universe was telling me to work on relationships—my relationship with myself; my relationship with my family, loved ones, and friends; my professional relationships; and my relationship with my creator.

Every new challenge, circumstance, situation, or experience brings either a new face to an old, underlying issue or a new issue to the same old, familiar face. Each small step willingly or unwillingly made in progress reveals more steps to come. Like the peeling of an onion, there is one layer after another, and each layer makes me cry. This is not a Western culture trip to a destination; this is an Eastern culture journey of a lifetime. If it ends, beware—you're probably dead. This is agonizing, torturous work that requires honesty with oneself, openness to new ideas and ways of thinking, and the willingness to be torn down and rebuilt. All I can say is that the pain of going through the process and reaping the rewards far outweighs the pain of sitting stuck, where I was all torn up. If I was torn up either way, I may as well get rebuilt. I am going to present some tough concepts about relationships as they were presented to me.

Honesty, Self-worth, and Trust

Honesty

Let's start with honesty. Am I honest? Honest with myself, with others, and with my creator. I do not mean to ask whether I am truthful. I am asking if I am honest. Truth is simply telling my truth as I see it. Honesty is revealing the true me. Honesty is the foundation of a healthy relationship, whether it is a relationship with someone else or my creator. If there is no honesty, there really is no relationship at all. My experience is that it is very difficult to be honest with myself, and if I do not get honest with myself, then I will not be capable of an honest relationship with anyone else. We broke our honesty with ourselves at one time or another because we felt compelled to avoid or get out of something we did not want to experience, and then that avoidance became a habit that drove more dishonesty. Honesty and fear go hand in hand. I cannot be honest if I live afraid. What could I be afraid of, and how could it possibly be worse than breaking my honesty with myself?

We are all familiar with the proverbial getting caught with our hand in the cookie jar. There I am, the stool moved over to the counter so that I can reach, the lid is off the cookie jar, my hands and mouth have chocolate all over them from the cookies and my mouth is so full of cookies that I can barely denounce the accusatory, "Did you get into the cookie jar?" with a resounding no. What would possess me to tell an obviously stupid and outrageous lie? It was the passing inspiration that perhaps the seemingly momentary lapse of truth would be less painful then the end of Dad's belt. It sounds so silly, but we do it all the time. We may get more sophisticated about it as we grow older, but we never get less stupid about it until we get honest with ourselves.

It is difficult for me to be honest with you right now. You are not just a stranger I will probably never meet. You are my family, friends, and loved ones. You are people with whom I live, pray, and work. Being honest with you means being transparent with you; it means showing you the real me. It means stepping out from behind the me I created in order to be the me I think you want me to be, so that you'd like me. This honesty is a level of transparency that leaves me vulnerable. Vulnerable to whether you like me or think of me as nuts. Vulnerable to your criticism or maybe even vulnerable to you appreciating me for the journey I share with you.

Let me paint a familiar picture. I like you, but I get afraid you will not like me, and so I get dishonest with myself and pretend I do not like you. By pretending I do not like you, you do not like me in return. And so by not being honest with myself about liking you, I have missed out of the opportunity of knowing you. I have attracted my own reality. I see this behavior on the playground of a preschool, and it is completely out of control by puberty in middle school. If not put in check, we continue this behavior in our adult lives—in the work place, in our social settings, and even in our churches.

When I was very young, my father ran a movie theater on weekends. He kept in his bedroom a cash box for this business. My brother was six years older than I, and he threatened to beat me up if I did not steal the money from this cash box. When I did, I was dishonest with myself by thinking he would spare me. Instead, he beat me up and took the money. When my father found out the money was missing, I was dishonest with him and said I did not take it, thinking I would avoid his belt. But my brother told Dad that I took it and claimed that when I gave it to him, he did not know it was stolen. He returned the money to Dad and looked like a hero. Again I was dishonest when I told Dad the whole truth, for fear of my brother's wrath. These kinds of warped mind games haunted my entire childhood because I could not be honest with myself, my brother, or my father.

By not being honest with myself and my dad, I gave power to my brother, which he used and abused. If I had been honest, I would have taken this power away from him—and with it his ability to intimidate and manipulate me. Today I have the self-worth to be honest and not give

The Fall of My Life

this kind of power to any friend, loved one, family member, or coworker. I have learned that not being honest does not avoid the situation; it only makes it worse. I have learned the freedom and empowerment that come with being honest.

The other lie we tell ourselves is that dishonesty only hurts us; we refuse to acknowledge how interconnected we all are. In the example where I liked you, my dishonesty with myself not only robbed me of the opportunity to get to know you, but it robbed you of the opportunity to get to know me. And who knows, maybe you liked me until you noticed our radio waves were not on the same frequency, and so you went off in the direction of someone else. How often do we see this scenario depicted in romantic movies without personalizing it. To quote a classic Don Maclean song, "You know I heard about people like me, but I never made the right connection. We walk one road to set us free, then we find we gone the wrong direction. But for me there is no turning back, because all roads lead to where I stand."

People who disobey helmet or seat belt laws and believe it is their right to get injured, dismembered, or killed are not being honest with the reality that their decisions and actions impact the ones they love and the public servants who witness these atrocities. People who have abused alcohol or drugs, once sober, are faced with the stark reality of how their actions have affected others, and they are challenged to make amends for those actions as part of a new honesty with themselves, others, and God. Careless, reckless, self-centered behavior is just a form of not being honest with ourselves.

I think the slyest form of dishonesty however is gossip. I have seen gossip destroy people, relationships, careers, and companies. When I choose to participate in something I hear about someone else, I choose to not be honest with at least three people, not counting God: myself, the gossiper, and the one being gossiped about. I would be devastated to learn that anyone else was talking about me the way that I talk about others, yet I do it because I lie to myself that no one is getting hurt. Don't be fooled. People are hurt by gossip every day. When I choose to participate in gossip, I unwittingly volunteer to be the victim of the next rumor.

Self-Worth

Next, let's discuss self-worth. Honesty and self-worth go hand in hand. A major component of self-worth is treating myself as worthy, and taking care of myself includes being honest with myself and protecting myself. It is both self-care and honesty to proactively protect myself from unnecessary risk. Toddlers learn this quickly when they touch something hot and get burned. They do not need to psychoanalyze it or rationalize it; they have come to understand in short order a simple cause and effect that they will not be repeating any time soon.

Some people are fortunate enough to have the awareness of their importance and value nourished. My perspective of myself was distorted because I was not aware of any feelings of self-worth, and I concealed my feelings of worthlessness by not showing warmth or concern for others. My doubt that I could ever do anything right, as well as the fear of change, graduated into self-hatred. I had to come to understand that even though I had made mistakes, I was still a worthwhile person. I eventually learned to respect myself for what I had lived through, and I began to appreciate my good qualities.

This principal is at the heart of why I had no close friends all the way through high school. In my formative years I had no compass or measuring stick, and so my perspective of myself was distorted—not what I could accomplish, but who I really was. Because I was uncertain of who I was, I had no self-worth. I tried to conceal that I felt worthless on the inside by not showing warmth or concern for anyone else. I reasoned that with my lack of appropriate tools, if I could keep people out, then they would not see what I thought was the real me. By keeping them out, I would not have to endure the pain and suffering of them rejecting me when they discover who I really was. By behaving this way, I imprisoned myself to solitary confinement and misery for over a decade.

But self-worth also includes setting my own standards for who I want to be, who and what I want to be around, and what I want to do. This applies to my family, friends, loved ones, and professional relationships. I make my own reality by the radio signals I send out. The radio signals I choose to emit come from my self-worth. Do I want to be in touch with my higher self and emit higher radio waves, or am I going to choose to remain stuck with my false self, emitting radios waves of doubt and lack? Being honest with myself and respecting myself gives me the foundation to define and create my own reality.

Trust

Finally, let's explore trust. When I do not trust myself or others, I do not trust God. Do I trust myself to not say yes when I mean no? This is the hardest one for me. Do I continue to trust someone who has violated my trust? When I do this, I find that I was not being honest with myself about that person or what he or she did to me. Do I trust God with the smallest details of my life? I would think I would know this by now, but I continue to not trust God even though he has faithfully proven himself repeatedly and without fail.

I learned a very powerful lesson over the last four years about trust. I was suspicious of a loved one's honesty, and I shared this with my sage. He informed me that if I did not trust her, I did not trust God. God has a perfect plan for my life, independent of her actions or behavior. Regardless of whether or not she is honest, God still has a perfect plan for me. In fact, that perfect plan may be realized in whether she is honest, or it could be realized in her dishonesty. By not trusting her, I was not trusting God. I put my trust in God, and my suspicion vanished. Honestly!

Motivation

What is my motivation in relationships? I found this question to be particularly slippery in the job search. I am adding motivation to my list of topics as a form of trust. Especially in the building of relationships in the job search, motivation played a key role in my success. When I talked about being a resource to others, having coffee with them, and them wanting to help me, this was not some twisted reserve psychology plot. I did not have a hidden agenda or ulterior motives. At one point along the way I had to ask myself the question that I ask you now: would you foster this relationship if you knew ahead of time it would never lead to a job?

Think about it. I mentioned before that if a relationship is not give and take, then it is not a relationship. All give or all take does not make a relationship. But what about when I am a resource (give), and what I get in return is feeling good for being a resource (take)? I do not get anything tangible in return. What if I give people leads that land them a jobs, and they never return my phone calls afterward? Was that a waste of my time? I am here to tell you that in my experience, it is not. I never know what I do not know. I never know what is going to lead to what.

I heard a young recruiter and career coach speak once about prioritizing his contacts in order of influence and what they could do for him. His justification was that in his line of work, he could not possibly foster all the relationships that came across his path. Perhaps in his line of work that is true, but I could not help but wonder what experiences he was missing out on because he was not allowing uncertainty to unfold.

If I am building relationships simply to get something in return, I will succeed in just that. My radio waves of "give me, give me" will be answered by the radio waves on the same frequency, and the universe will take; I will attract other people that are building relationships only to get something in return. I said that when I first attended networking events, I did not care about anyone else; I was only looking for someone who could get me a job. A short time later, as I was growing up in my true understanding of networking, a very young girl frantically approached me with her stack of resumes, held one out for me to take, and asked me if I was a recruiter. When I smiled and nearly laughed at her, she retracted the offer of the resume and scurried away like a squirrel looking for nuts. Not a "Hello," "What's your name," "My name is . . ." "Good-bye," or "Thank you." I stood there dumbfounded. But I had gotten back what I'd put out.

"Yuk"

I was determined I would not be like that again. I need to be a resource to build relationships. This radio frequency will attract other people who want to be a resource, and we will find each other. We will build meaningful and fulfilling relationships instead of shallow and dishonest relationships. I will boost my self-worth, I will increase my energy level, I will be more attractive to others, and I will attract what I want in my life. My inner circle that started out with me and my dog now includes dozens of close friends whom I know and love. They are friends with whom I am honest, whom I trust, and for whom I have pure motives. You can, too.

On the reverse end of the spectrum are other people's motives. When I had ulterior motives, I was not trustworthy of other people's motives. I had to reflect on my friends and acquaintances and take stock of my and their motivations, and then I realigned my reality. When my motives are pure, I do not need to get caught up in the mind games about whether someone else's motives are pure. Even if a person's motives are not pure, if mine are, then everything will work out in the end. Good things will always come out of bad things if my motives are aligned with the reality that I want to attract.

Judgments and Assumptions

I briefly touched on this earlier, but it requires a lot more attention. Do I judge you because you make more or less money than I, are older or younger, dress better or worse, drive a more expensive car, or own a bigger house? Do I assume you are smarter than I am because you are a CEO, are the owner of your own business, or have titles connected to your name? Do I judge you because of the music you like, the skateboard you ride, or the fact that you smoke? Do I assume you are less intelligent because you are homeless, younger, overweight, blonde, or a myriad other excuses? The answer is that yes, I do.

Judgments and assumptions hold us back and cripple us. My recruiter friend judges who he thinks is influential, and he assumes they can get him what he wants. He is unknowingly missing out on those he judged could not help him. The young gal at the networking event assumed that only a recruiter could help her. If I was not as she judged and could not help her as she assumed, then I did not deserve to even know her name. She missed out on the opportunity to get to know me, she robbed me of the opportunity to get to know her, she missed out on the "Bob factor," and I am guessing that unless she changed her course, she is still looking for a job.

Having no judgments and no assumptions means that I do not know what I do not know. Does this ring a bell? It means I do not know who knows who. I went to an interview once, and both the hiring manager and I agreed the position was not right for me, but he liked me and knew an acquaintance he thought could help me. That acquaintance did not have a job, but he knew another acquaintance that did. I wound up getting the interview through the third acquaintance. Even though his opportunity did not qualify as my dream job either, it was an amazing journey of meeting and chatting with a series of folks that, just like me, were operating from a place of no judgments and no assumptions.

The point is, who would have thought? I have countless other stories of how approaching a person or situation with an open mind leaves me open to possibilities that I would otherwise miss out on. This applies to my personal as well as my professional life. Saying yes to possibilities is saying yes to life. Living life to its fullest is saying yes to God. Saying yes to God is the ultimate source of fulfillment and happiness. Having no judgments or assumptions creates my own reality, the reality I want. I won't get the reality I want if I get blocked by judgments and assumptions. I judge that you know what I mean by now and I assume you do know that I mean.

The final concept I want to discuss about relationships comes from a little book called *The Four Agreements* by Don Miguel Ruiz. The first agreement is, "Say what you mean, mean what you say, and don't be mean when you say it." If you want to know what the other agreements are, you will have to read the book. If I could live just this one agreement, my life would be so much easier. All the themes of this book are interwoven throughout this single, simple concept; fear, reality, intention, attraction, self-worth, honesty, trust, and motivation are all packed into this agreement. This is my journey in one sentence, applied to all my interactions with myself, my world, and my God.

Let's break it down. "Say what you mean." I am talking to a loved one, and I am coming from a place of fear and say something I do not mean. I have injured myself, her, and God. I am in my car, and another driver does something I do not appreciate. I am coming from a place of anger, so I pass on a form of nonverbal communication that I do not mean. I have just emitted radio waves that will attract similar radio waves. I am at work and choose to participate in a "Did you hear what she said . . . ?" conversation. I have just created the strong possibility that I will be the subject of the tomorrow's gossip. These are three examples of not saying what I mean, and each is equally poignant.

"Mean what you say." A friend asks me if I would like to join him for a movie tonight, and I say yes. I really want to stay home and watch reruns of *I Love Lucy,* but I don't tell him that. My boss asks me if I have time to finish this project by the end of the day, and I say yes when in fact there is no way on God's green earth that I can get that project done by the end of the day—but I can't tell her that. God asks me if I am willing to do whatever it takes, and I say yes just to get him off my back, but I know that when push comes to shove, I will not.

"Don't be mean when you say it." Or in my case, don't be sarcastic. This is hard to do, especially when highly rated television shows and popular movies are overflowing with every possible form of mean and sarcastic communication. This reinforces my brain to think that this is okay. It is not okay—it is demeaning. I get told frequently how I harm: I do not mean intentional harm, but I harm nonetheless. Words are powerful and dangerous; they can heal and they can destroy. I aspire to learn and master this third component of this concept.

Let's put it all back together now. "No, I have other plans tonight, but I would love to some other time. Thank you for asking." I do not need to apologize or rationalize;

I am creating my own reality. I said what I meant, I meant what I said, and I was not mean when I said it. Now, if I could just actually *do* that. Let's try it again, and maybe we will get better with practice. "Actually, I am trying to get this other project done before my Tai Chi lesson tonight. Do I need to stop working on this project and finish that project, or can it wait until tomorrow?" Who has the guts to say that to his or her boss? No hands? Me neither.

There is a book by Ernest Kurtz and Katherine Ketcham called *The Spirituality of Imperfection*. The theme of this book sums up what I have tried to share about my journey with respect to relationships. Everybody is on a journey. Relationships are all about touching another human being in a positive way as we cross paths on our own unique journeys. Loving and accepting people just as they are, wherever they are—this is life. No judgments and no assumptions. You are who you are in your place, and I am who I am in mine.

I remember hearing an interview once with a great baseball player. I do not remember who the interviewer or the baseball player was, but it does not matter—it is what he said that matters. The interviewer asked him what his secret was to being one of the greatest athletes ever, and he answered, "There are some things that I am good at and other things I am not so good at. I practice on the ones I am not so good at until I am good at them." That is my inspiration in relationships. There are some things that I am already good at and other things I haven't got good at yet. I practice on the ones I haven't got good at yet so that I may get good at them too.

I had been working hard at my professional career for over thirty years with a mentality that work and home were two separate boxes. I thought of it as work-life balance. When I was at work, I work; I did not socialize or fraternize. When I am at home, I did not work. I was missing out on not only enjoying the hundreds of people I have worked with throughout my career, but also letting them get to know and enjoy me.

Several years ago, this concept hit me upside the head like a two by four, but at the time I did not know what to do about it. I was discussing a year-end performance review with my manager. I had shattered all my goals for the year, and they were very specific and measurable, so he was trying to explain to me why I was not going to get a raise that year. In short, he said, "Because you piss everybody off." I decided *they* were the problem, and I got a job somewhere else. He was attempting to get me to understand that *how* I do it is just as important as what I do. Fifteen years later, I was looking for a job again, and I finally began to understand what he was trying to say.

Today I have learned that the relationships I have with the people whom I spend sixty hours a week with are actually the most important part of what I do in the job I have. I am now genuinely interested in my coworkers. When I ask them how they are or what they did over the weekend, I actually mean it. I have developed the self-worth to open myself up at work and share a little bit about my personal life. I have prayed, hugged, said "I love you," cried, and laughed with my coworkers. Now that I have experienced the new Bob, I wish this for everyone.

I hope that sharing my journey though relationships with you will inspire you, too. I once heard from a wise, old sage that the ultimate relationship is when you not only accept someone for who and where they really are in their imperfections, but you love them *because of* their imperfections. When you figure that one out, let me know—I am still working on it.

Chapter 7

The Rest of the Story

"Mama always said life was like
a box of chocolates . . ."
—*Forrest Gump*

The Fall of My Life

In true, old-fashioned, Paul Harvey spirit, I am sure by now you are wondering, "what job did you get, how did you get it, and what's up with this boss of yours". Let's start with the how. It was late June 2010, nearing two years after the failure of WaMu. I was in the peak of my informational interviews and networking events. I was particularly interested in an opportunity at a small business in Seattle. I knew a former WaMu associate who knew the owner of one, and so I scheduled a time to chat about this company. I had indirectly reported to this associate on a project in the last months of WaMu. Over the course of the last two years, we had developed a personal relationship as well.

Now, there is one very important thing to know about this person. She has created her own reality by, in her words, "Assuming as is" at both a personal and professional level. Professionally, when WaMu failed, she did not miss a heartbeat. She is a leader who, when she was a follower, paid very close attention to where she was being led. She was never unemployed. The first reality she created was a significant place for herself with a large, global enterprise. The second reality she created was being allowed to work out of a satellite office in Seattle. The third reality she created for herself was creating a staff largely made up of former WaMu employees.

I met with her, and we talked about what I wanted to talk about. Then we started talking about her latest situation at work. As she was describing a monstrous new change coming, she froze in her chair, sat straight up like she had seen a ghost, looked at me, and said, "You are the solution to my problem." I felt like I was in one of those comic strips where the person gets an idea, and there is a light bulb over her head. We talked about it in a little more detail, and then my scheduled time was up.

Even though this was very exciting news for a lot of different reasons, the number one rule of the job hunt is to not stop hunting until after you have started the new job. Too many things fall apart at the last minute. I personally know of one person who was offered a new job and injured himself the weekend before he was to start. When he called in for what was supposed to be his first day on the new job, and he told them he had injured himself and needed to go to the doctor, they told him to not bother reporting to work. Yes this is a true story. I swear it.

So I continued to go about my business doing informational interviews and networking events, and I even got a couple of other interviews for pretty good positions and made it to the final round of candidates. In the meantime, I continued to check in with her, and she with me, regarding the progress of her idea for me. I was entertained that as I got close to be offered jobs a couple of times, she became very anxious that she was going to lose me. But none of those jobs were meant to be, as we would both soon learn. Weeks went by as I watched the idea materialize into PowerPoint presentations and organizational charts. It wasn't until October that the idea had fully taken form and was now in the approval stages with the company.

While all this was transpiring, I was getting financially worse off by the month. My unemployment check did not even cover my basic bills, and I had been paying portions of my rent late for months now. This was when I was pulling weeds. When I was done being on my knees all day, I could hardly walk, but I showered and went to my networking events anyway. In September I did not know how much more of this I could physically bear, and then I got my answer: I was issued an eviction notice from my landlord—not for failure to pay rent, but for failure to pay a five-dollar late fee after I had paid the rent late. This was my rock bottom.

I was angry. I was very angry! First of all, I conveniently didn't know about the late fee. Like I said, I had been making portions of the rent payment late for months and had never gotten a late fee before. But more important, really now, couldn't he just knock on the door or pick up the phone and ask for the five dollars? Were we really going to do this?

I called my sage, and my reality changed. I had to own up to my part. I had been paying rent late and risking this enforcement action. In the end I paid the five dollars and kept my mouth shut. Although I will never agree with how the landlord handled this situation, my reality is that I can only control and change me.

Upon a closer look at this situation after I calmed down, I realized I was angry because I was living in fear. I was afraid of being homeless. I was coming from a place of shortage and lack. I was not trusting God and was attracting everything I did not want. It was time for me to align my thinking with my intention. It was time for me to create my own reality and attract what I wanted. This was my turning point. This was when that big ball of trouble and disappointments that had been hanging over my head, blocking the sun's warm rays like a storm cloud, shattered and transformed into beautiful glitter.

After I told enough friends about this situation, a small group of them conspired to provide me with odd jobs behind a desk through October so that I would not be in so much pain, and I could pay the rent. Then in November, a primary character in this story arranged for me a contract job for two weeks of significant pay at her company. It was legitimate work that she needed done; she would have had to hire someone else for it anyway, but it saved me. It saved me physically and it saved me financially. My reality was beginning to take shape.

In December I started working in my new job for my new boss, who had created a hand-tailored job for me. That is how I got the job. If I had not extended the energy to foster this relationship, I would not have been there in that moment when she decided I was the answer to her problem; someone else would have been on her mind as she contemplated her dilemma. I fostered this relationship not because I judged her as influential or because I assumed she could get me a job, but because she knew how to attract her reality, I was learning how to attract my reality, and so our radio waves aligned. My intention to get the job that I wanted matched her intention to secure an employee that would attract what she had decided she wanted.

I had been focusing on what I was attracting into my life for some time now, but it is important to understand that one cannot turn a ship around on a dime. The negative, self-defeating radio signals I had been transmitting for years were still out there and coming back to me, while at the same time I was transmitting new, positive, affirming powerful radio signals, but they were only on their way out, looking for matching signals. During this time the universe in my life was in upheaval. A new job was being created while I was being evicted. Temporary and contract jobs were being created, and ultimately my new job was created. I was now attracting the signals for the life I was creating for myself.

This new job was not just a new job. It was the culmination of the hard work that I had done over the last four years to have a new experience with myself, my world, and God. It was the perfect alignment of the radio waves I had transmitted out to the universe, to attract new people and experiences aligned with the new me that I had reinvented. As the next two years unfolded, I slowly grew more aware of just how significant this new season of my life was. The new me was born, but only born—it still needed to develop and grow up to an adult.

I recently saw a documentary about the 1983 NCAA men's championship basketball team at North Carolina State and their coach, Jim Valvano. Valvano had accepted the head coach position at NC State four years earlier, along with a talented group of freshman recruits. He told everyone who would listen that he was going the win the NCAA championship; he repeatedly pronounced this acclimation to his team. With the team, he even went to the extreme of practicing cutting down the nets, which is the tradition at the end of this tournament victory. He explained to them that they have to do it to experience it. He was not just trying to motivate his team, even though he did a historically unbelievable job at it—he actually believed it.

During his first year as head coach, this team did not even make it to the tournament. The following two years birthed appearances in the tournament but ended with disappointments. In 1983, no one other than Coach Valvano gave NC State a chance at winning a national championship. His team stormed through the tournament, creating one

The Fall of My Life

last-second heroic victory after another over higher ranked teams with better season records. They ultimately won what is still considered to be the greatest upset in college basketball history.

Coach Valvano delivered an equally remarkable motivational speech ten years later at the ESPY Awards, eight weeks before he died of cancer. In this speech he talked about the source of his confidence to win the national championship against all odds: his father. He revealed how his father has always believed in him and had never criticized him. He told about how during those four years that stamped his name in the history books, each time he declared to his father that he was going to win the national championship, his father's reply was always an affirmative: "My bags are packed. I will be there." This confidence poured out into his team. Throughout the documentary on Jim and his team, there were interviews with the now adult roster of that championship team. They all echoed the resounding opinion that at first they thought he was crazy, but slowly over those four years, they internalized his confidence as their own, and they pulled off the impossible.

My new boss was my Coach V. She was not just a motivator or fast talker—although she was that, too. She was an inspiration to her team because she actually believed; she "assumed as." She practiced cutting down the net. She started at the end and created her own reality. She aligned her dreams with the universe. As I began working under her authority, I sought to learn how to emulate her approach and practices to herself, the world around her, and the workplace. I began to know and understand what I was capable of, and I came to believe that we could win the national championship.

Now, don't get me wrong: I am not putting anyone up on a pedestal. My boss was not perfect; she had her own flaws. We had disagreements, misunderstandings, and conflict, the worst of which, for me, was a moment when I was particularly frustrated and was expressing my feelings about it online to a peer of mine when I accidentally sent the message to her instead of him. I was mortified and physically nauseous. She called me. I confessed, apologized, and told her how badly I felt. She listened, and the situation made both our professional and personal relationship stronger. A lesser person would have not handled the situation as gracefully. This incident opened my eyes to how prevalent this behavior was in the workplace, and so I challenged myself to not participate anymore as an initiator or observer.

I am not saying that I have become mystically perfect. At the time of this incident, I managed thirteen people, and I am quite sure any one of them could readily rattle off a list of my shortcomings. But my boss emulated the kind of boss I wanted to be: one with integrity and character above all else. She inspired and motivated me to care for and serve people as a leader. I experienced the fruits of my efforts on several occasions, when I received very personal, heartfelt messages from employees expressing their gratitude for me as a leader and for the manner in which I managed and treated them with transparency and honesty. I received priceless feedback of how I had motivated and inspired them as well. I had become better.

I mentioned in the foreword that what inspired me to write this book was the urging of the friends I have built relationships with over the last five years. When I decided to take this urging seriously—primarily because I could not ignore them any longer—I did a little homework to find out what it would really take to get this book into your hands, so that I knew what I was getting myself into. Shortly after I had done my homework and decided I was all in, I was abruptly woke wide awake in the middle of the night in a cold sweat with the title of the book figuratively speaking tattooed to my forehead, *The Fall of My Life*. It was the trifecta of everything I once knew being destroyed while the financial markets collapsed in the autumn years of my life, and my subsequent journey of molding a new me.

Over the ensuing months, I experienced several other involuntary, inspirational sound bites that slowly formulated into an outline and the remaining contents of this book. The perfect beach cottage setting to write this book, the artist who drew up the cover, the editors who helped shape a manuscript into publishable material, and the publisher who guided me through the foreign process were all serendipitous occurrences of a force greater than I, fitting all the pieces together to put this book into your hands. I am honored and grateful to have had the experience of sharing my journey with you.

    And that . . . is the rest of the story.

Chapter 8

The Next Chapter

"Everything will be all right in the end, and if it's not all right, then it's not yet the end."
—*The Best Exotic Marigold Hotel*

Now that it was 2011, and I had secured yet another job in the financial services industry. I became more cognizant of the lingering, negative sentiment toward financial institutions, and reasonable so. When you hear that the current unemployment rate is 7.6 percent, understand that translates to 11.7 million of the current US work force in the United States. The unemployment rate peaked in May 2010 at 9.9 percent; that means that over 15 million people lost their jobs during the "Great Recession". Today 40 percent of those unemployed have been so for over two years. Given how many have remained jobless even after their unemployment benefits expired, the true number of unemployed today is estimated to be at least twice that, if not triple that.

Of those who have become employed again, it is estimated that three-fifths of them accepted lower paying jobs, just to have a job. In addition, many of those that managed to keep their jobs still suffered crippling financial losses of homes, retirement funds, and investments. The resentment in the air on the street corner where the average American stands still begs the question, "When is someone going to go to jail for the losses I sustained?" Five years later, America is still mad, sad, worried, and frustrated. Americans are still waiting for someone to pay. American is still waiting for justice to be served.

I would like to devote this chapter to talking to you about what it is like be one of the six million people who work inside the financial services industry. Regardless of how it looks and feels from the outside, seeing financial services institutions be given handouts from our government and continue to roll-out profits quarter after quarter, inside those institutions are mostly people just like you and I, working their hardest to do the right thing. I assure you that the general public's hostility is felt by most of our elected officials, who pressure our federal regulators, who pressure our financial industry leaders, who in turn pressure my colleagues and me.

The first year of my life at my new job had been filled with challenges. It was now time to translate the principals I had learned during the job-hunting phase of my life into performing well on the job. I was tested and stretched in ways I never had been before on the job. Just as my job was created for me, a major component of my job became the responsibility to create and build a new team. Of course, things are never as they appear. As it turned out, I hired thirteen employees across three very distinct teams. Decisions come slowly and awkwardly in a very large company, so most of the time I felt like I was keeping a sinking ship afloat, bailing out water, and patching holes while I was building a new, bigger, and better ship. I worked eighty to one hundred hours a week the first half of that year. Nonetheless, I ended the year with the teams in place. I had accomplished far more than I'd set out to do.

It was nine months before my teams were fully in place. As I mentioned in the chapter on mechanics, I had hired all them upon personal referral; all but one had held previous positions with the company. I emulated my boss's habit of holding weekly staff meetings. In my weekly staff calls, I promoted transparency and honesty. I saw my role as making sure each employee had all the necessary tools to do his or her job. I consider complete and timely information to be one of those essential tools for success. I ended each meeting with a personal touch: I left them with an inspirational or motivational quote for the week. Many of these employees had come from other parts of the company that were not managed in my style. They repeatedly expressed their gratitude and devotion because they were no longer enduring an hostile work environment and toxic personnel issues. I was horrified to hear the stories about how people had been abused and repressed.

At one meeting I decided to share a personal experience. I had just gotten two tattoos. My journey to acquire these tattoos had not come as a result of a drunken stupor, as so many do. My tattoo transpired the hard way, as does everything I seem to do; it slowly developed through much thought and study. I had decided twenty years ago that I wanted to get one, but I wanted it to be a very deep and meaningful expression of my innermost self. I decided ten years ago that I wanted it to be a Chinese symbol, born out of my blossoming interest in Eastern culture, philosophy, and spirituality. One day it hit me out of the blue: I knew what I wanted, and I did it the next day. The result was on my left shoulder I got the Chinese symbol for "dream," and on my right shoulder I got the Chinese symbol for "big." Together it reads, "Dream big."

(Not until I wrote these very words did the serendipitous significance hit me. Because it took me a year to write this book, by the time I got these tattoos, I had completely forgotten that the first of the three simple steps of reality I had shared with you in chapter four was, "Dream big.")

This simple exposure of a small piece of my life journey created an even deeper sense of appreciation from my employees. Whether real or perceived, I felt that another important aspect of my job was relationships, Relationships with my employees, my peers, my stakeholders, and my superiors. We were all working at a blistering pace, and people's worst behaviors come out when they are stressed. My journey these past five years would had been in vain had I not been able to practice the very principles I had been learning. I had endeavored to be honest and trustworthy in all my interactions, to check my motivations at the door, and to treat everyone without judgment or assumptions. In short, I wanted to lead with integrity, the way my boss did.

Of particular significance was a myriad of new processes that needed to be established around this new function I was now a part of and managing. This task was full of land mines. People's patience was low, emotions were high, and resistance to change held its typical place in the minds and attitudes of most people. I was responsible for both the change and the management of the change. I built powerful alliances by treating people with respect and patience while at the same time demonstrating my mastery of process change and pushing the process forward.

For me, an important part of this first year had been two major surgeries. Health insurance is wonderful. Nine months after I was literally on my knees, I was granted the modern miracle of a toe fusion surgery on my left foot and a knee replacement on my right leg. I was able to continue my work from home during the difficult rehabilitation process, but in a few short months I was physically renewed. I remember when I was finally able to return to the office, and my boss noticed that I did not limp anymore. I told her, "You have to understand that before this surgery, I had not taken a step without pain for thirty-five years."

The year 2011 drew to a conclusion with the excitement and challenge of a new job—just in time to present me with a new and exciting challenge. I had devoted another year of my life to creating my own reality. I had sent out positive, constructive radio waves of intention to get what I wanted out of life, and I was attracting like radio waves. When the year-end performance review process was executed I was recognized for my contributions to the company. I was identified as a top performer in my boss's team, and I earned the privilege of a promotion. My most rewarding moment of the year was not a single one of my many accomplishments. It was hearing my boss tell me during the performance review, "You are just not the same person you were a year ago."

Then the unthinkable happened. Executive management decided that there would be no raises and no promotions this year; the excuse they used was the Occupy Wall Street movement. I felt as if I had been kicked in the stomach and was gasping to catch my breath. Everyone across the organization was in shock. I was angry. My inner spirit knew that this was not an acceptable way for an employer to treat an employee, especially a top performer. I searched my soul while trying to create a workplace of calm and security for my employees and peers.

I took vacation time over the year-end holidays to absorb this blow. I talked to my friends and my perspective was challenged. On the one hand, I already made a sizable income associated with my education and experience, and it was above what most of my friends made, so they did not grant me a lot of sympathy. On the other hand, I was most certainly not the Wall Street fat cat 1 percent that the Occupy Movement was targeting. This seemed to me to be a clear abuse of power by the 1 percent. It was not fair and it was not right, but in the end none of that mattered.

When top management heard the battle cries of the working class over the next few weeks, they retaliated with the twisted logic that we were all lucky to still have jobs and maintain our compensation levels; many other Wall Street firms were laying people off or cutting compensation. Although these statements were partially true, they were nothing short of a continuation of abuse of authority through threat and intimidation.

Before I got too political, I spent the remainder of my time off in prayer and meditation. How was my higher self, going to respond to this atrocity? The first reality was that I couldn't control what had happened. By letting go of the illusion of control over other people and their actions, I found an enormous burden was lifted, and I began to discover the freedom and the power I possessed. When I exerted the power to define my life on my terms, my personal unmanageability lessened, and I took back the ability to manage my own life. I was powerless over others, but that did not make me helpless. I did my best with what I had at the time. I was not going to be able to argue this issue and change anyone's mind, so I was left only with the decision of how I was going to respond. How *did* I want to respond? When all was said and done on this subject, what did I want people to remember about Bob?

I started my mini journey. I was angry, so let's take a look at that. I was angry because I was afraid, and I was afraid because I was living in lack. Let me explain. Consider that at fifty-five, I was materially and financially starting all over from zero. I had within my intention to own my own home and retire on a comfortable income. One thing I did to attract that intention was set up a financial plan with a professional that achieves these goals. Now my financial plan was upset, and I was afraid I would not achieve my goals of owning and retiring.

I had to adjust my thinking. My financial plan was not my reality; my employer was not my God. God had a financial plan of abundance and prosperity for me, and that was my reality. I blew up my financial plan, my fear went away, and my anger turned into serenity. That was how it worked. I sat down with my financial planner, and we wrote a new financial plan more in line with God's plan—and may I add, it was a better plan.

But I still felt taken advantage of by my employer, so let's take a look at that. I am sure there are millions of employees across the globe that feel the same way, particularly in these uncertain economic times. I felt taken advantage of because I had a reasonable expectation that I would be fairly compensated for my contribution to the company. But I agreed to take my job at the compensation that was offered, and nobody made me any promises or signed any contracts that it would ever change. I based my expectation on historical patterns of past employers. So was my expectation fair? Did it matter if Joe or Sally made more or less than me, if I was the one who agreed to what I make?

Expectations are premeditated resentments, and my resentment was not going to hurt my employer—it was only going to eat me alive. If I wanted to live in peace with myself, I had a choice to make: acceptance or action. Did I stay where I was at the compensation I agreed to, or did I find another job at the compensation I wanted and felt I was worthy of? That presented two questions: could I, and was I willing to. Could I really get a job somewhere else for more money? Was I really willing to initiate a job hunt again?

For me, the answers to those two questions were buried in more questions. My insides felt like a bad sci-fi movie. Could I get a better job? I didn't know. Ironically, later on another financial services institution approached me, completely unsolicited. I was one of the final two candidates for a position that would have paid me what I believed I was worth on the market. I had to do a great deal of soul searching over this opportunity. I told them that I if I had to prioritize, I would choose culture over money because I already had the culture I wanted where I was, and I would not leave that just for more money. However, I would leave my job for both culture and money. As it turned out, they selected the other candidate. I came to the conclusion that the bigger question was more important to me: did I want to? It was time to take stock in what I had. It was time to get my gratitude back, because except for this little compensation issue that I created with my own false expectations, this was my dream job, managing my dream team and working for my dream boss. My job and my boss were what I attracted with my intention, and I was the employee that my boss attracted with her intention. When I worded it that way, it sounded like the universe would explode if I tampered with it.

Let's get real. I had a boss I was aligned with spiritually. She treated all her employees the way they should be treated, with dignity and respect. I aspired to be the kind of manager to my employees that she was to hers. She gave me opportunities and challenged me to grow. She recognized me for my accomplishments and coached me on my weak points. She set an example and mentored me in my career path. In short, she had what I wanted. How many people can make a statement like that about their bosses? Where else was I going to find all this?

This was the job I'd spent two years trying to get. I would not walk away from it or hang around with a bad attitude. I returned to my job at the beginning of 2012 with

The Fall of My Life

a renewed vigor and perspective. I was all in, and I told my boss as much. I was creating my own reality. I was attracting what I intended, and I was encouraged that she was, too. I remained committed to understanding problems and to solving them by delivering results and being willing to be held accountable for them. Since this decision, I had been given additional responsibilities, my staff continued to grow, and I was facing new challenges and opportunities to contribute, learn, and grow every day.

During the first quarter of 2012, an employee who worked for my boss's boss left her position, creating a new opportunity for me. This position was more in line with most of my career path, and I volunteered to be considered. He agreed to assign the work to me, but it had to be in addition to the responsibilities I already performed, and I continued to report to my current boss. He would pursue recognizing the promotion I had already earned, but he could make no promises. In turn, I drafted the members of my management team into the pursuit of this new endeavor as we struggled to deliver a value-added product for him on top of our current tasks. In the ensuing months, a new senior executive began a complete reorganization of his entire team, and my promotion was ignored in the chaos.

As the second quarter of the year unfolded, we began to see a restructure of biblical proportions, beginning with my boss being stripped of all her responsibilities—and I lost most of the team I had built. Now, remember that I had lived through nine company failures up to this point in my career, so when I use the term of biblical proportions, I mean it. I had never seen anything like this. Hundreds of employees from other parts of the company were being drafted into our organization. My boss, the three remaining members of my team, and I regrouped to provide my boss's boss with the operational support that he needed in this environment, but shortly thereafter he was also stripped of all his responsibilities.

We watched in shock and awe as a recognized leader throughout the industry and an executive of eight senior leaders responsible for hundreds of jobs was replaced. Before the year was over, half his senior team was also replaced, and at the time of this writing, the other half has had their responsibilities reduced. A new management team equipped with swarms of employees quickly arrived and swiftly absorbed their newly appointed responsibilities, just like the day that Chase showed up at the WaMu headquarters only four years earlier. They put in place a new infrastructure of armies for what only a handful of us had previously been managing.

As I observed this transforming activity, I rapidly came to one conclusion. I needed (and wanted) to be in New York, where all the action was. I presented such a proposition to one senior manager of the new regime and was invited for a one-month trial period. This was essentially an on-the-job application for a new position and the promotion I'd continued to attract. In my first week there, I felt the enormous burden of how in demand my historical knowledge and skill set was. I was asked to continue to support my old boss and her boss, and I was asked to support a new, emerging senior leader—all while I was trying out for the senior leader who had brought me to New York. I was serving three masters. I was jack of all trades and master of none. I started a new project every day and sometimes more, but I was never able to bring anything across the finish line. I quickly saw this as a no-win situation.

That first month was my first real New York experience. The stereotypes and generalizations did not prove to be true for me. First of all, outside of work on the streets at night and after a long day, I never felt in danger. The entire time I spent in New York, I only encountered one person I thought was very rude. Also, outside of work I made the best of my situation and took advantage of the splendid themes that many people pay good money to go to New York to see and do. I drove out to Cape Cod one weekend. I took the Circle Tour of Manhattan via boat. I went to Central Park in the fall, and I went ice skating there at Christmas time. I visited Chinatown, the Brooklyn Bridge, Greenwich Village, and the awe-inspiring cathedrals. I saw the Rockets and a show at the Apollo, and I visited a number of sports bars to participate in college and NLF football mania.

I thoroughly enjoyed my time in New York and was willing to move there for the promotion I continued to attract. I was born and raised in the wheat fields of eastern Oregon. I remember when I moved away to go to college in the small town of Eugene, I thought at the time that I was moving to the big city. Five years later, I moved to Seattle seeking relief from the depressed employment market in Eugene, and I really felt like I was moving to the big city then. Upon my return to Seattle from New York, I recall thinking to myself how small Seattle now felt to me. So for me to be willing to move to New York, the mother of big cities, was a major statement.

Inside the office was an altogether different experience. The opportunity I had come to New York for slipped through my fingers because yet another wave of reform rippled through the organization, and the team I was trying out for completely imploded. Shortly after that, another senior leader recognized my contributions in the chaos of swarming activity; this provided me the opportunity to present her with the same one-month trial period proposition and another shot for the promotion I continued to attract. She reluctantly accepted, and I later learned it was nothing more than her seizing the opportunity to temporarily employ a warm body until she could transfer the person she really wanted into the position. He was hired, and I was asked to return to Seattle for good.

In one sense, this environment was no different than any one of the other companies I had worked for, both inside and outside the financial services industry. It seems that 99 percent of the employees are good people working hard to do the right thing, and 1 percent are not. The worst example of the 1 percent I have ever encountered was with a financial services company in the mid-eighties. The president, CEO, and chairman of the board had a reputation that I was unfortunate enough to have witnessed but fortunate enough to not have been the subject of his wrath. This man of top authority would actually scream at the top of his lungs, curse, demean, threaten, and belittle one member of his senior staff after another, and then he'd hysterically laugh at them, simply because he could.

Of course by the numbers, the larger a company is, the more people there are that represent the 1 percent. In this company there were many bad seeds. They manage by fear and intimidation and spread their imperfections like poison. I witnessed others of the 99 percent succumb to the cancerous behavior; they adopted the very actions and attitudes that hounded them down as examples were set and fear was instilled. They began to do things that they would not otherwise do if they had not been led down that path. I personally endured my way through lies, denial, taking credit for someone else's work, and claiming they did not say or do something. This behavior was as dysfunctional as my birth family, and it was the ultimate test of my newfound principals to live by.

By calling this book a journey, I am recognizing the most important principal in human relationships. We all start and end our journeys at different times and places. We are all going somewhere different. We all learn differently and at different paces on our journey. So how can I possibly expect everyone to be the same? How can I expect everyone to believe the same thing I believe, think the same thing or way, act the same, or feel the same? The notion is completely absurd, but I do it—we all do it. I went home every night and sometimes even had to take a walk around the block midday, searching for the right thing to do in that environment. I tried to understand what would drive people to such behavior besides an overwhelming sense of fear. I strove to look past the behaviors of people and address their real needs where they really were. I tried to not become like them. I tried to be different and stand out, not to further my career but to make my statement that people were more important than money.

I aligned with many exceptional people that I met while I was working in New York, and these people shared my values and joined me in striving to rise above the bad behavior. I formed allegiances with people I respected and

The Fall of My Life

connected with, not to further my career but to maintain my integrity and character. Together we reminded each other that relationships were the most important thing in a work place where we spent at least sixty hours a week of our lives. By building and fostering relationships with healthy people, I helped them in the same way they helped me: to not be like the 1 percent. I learned that more than in Seattle, many people lived in fear of losing their jobs in New York because so many other Wall Street firms were laying off or cutting compensation. This fear prevailed and sabotaged otherwise good people.

As I took the initiative to get to know select individuals on more than a superficial level, I learned about a couple of the life-changing events we in Seattle only saw on TV and read in the paper: 9/11 and Tropical Storm Sandi. People shared very personal stories with me about how 9/11 seared permanent images into their minds and altered their lives forever. I saw with my own eyes the hopelessness and helplessness that the victims of hurricane Sandi felt long after it was no longer a headline. There was nothing I could do but listen in amazement. I presumed that it was all I was intended to do—to listen. We have had it so good here in Seattle.

As 2013 rolled, in I learned that even though the promotion I had earned the previous year was once again fought against, it finally survived the darkness that had repeatedly suppressed it. At this point it felt anticlimactic, but I was nonetheless grateful for its finality. I also learned that the raise associated with this promotion was cut in half from what it was requested to be by my boss. Shortly afterward, my boss was laid off. They justified this atrocity by claiming the position had been eliminated. In over thirty years of professional employment, I had never witnessed a more senseless act against another competent person. As one would surmise, another company recognized my boss's value and awarded her by creating an even more senior position for her, just as she had done for me two years earlier.

After long deliberation and careful consideration, I decided that this environment was not for me. But I had made a mark at this company and preferred to stay employed within it, compared to looking for a new role outside the company. I sought advice from others who had been with the firm longer and had experienced other parts of the company. I made every attempt to seek out a corner where there might be the same culture that my boss had fostered two years ago with her team. With little effort on my part, I found such a place. I traveled twice to interview for a role that would have been an additional promotion for me in this new group. I made my way to the final two candidates, but in the end they did not offer me the position. I was dumbfounded and devastated to not get this role.

The Fall of My Life

There was a point I reached when it was just not working for me anymore, no matter how hard I tried or what I did. It was time for me to take stock of my career projectile. After my boss was laid off, all of the employees I'd hired found new jobs somewhere else in the firm. As for me, I wrote this book. Of all the races, games, and matches I have won; of all the certificates, ribbons and trophies I have awarded, this book is my greatest accomplishment. Of all the databases and spreadsheets I have built throughout my career; of all the graphs and reports I have produced and presented, this book is my greatest contribution. This book is the best thing I have ever done for myself. This book is why I am here, right now. If it were not for every single point that I stumbled over and cursed at, you would not have just read this book.

Epilogue

Somewhere along the way, I heard this story. A young man was walking along a path, and he came to a fork in the road. At the fork was an old man, so the young man asked the old man, "Which way should I go?" The old man replied, "Go to your right." So the young man went to the left. The young man's choice caused him much peril, and the young man ultimately wound up right back where he had started, at the same fork in the road where the same old man stood. So once again the young man asked the old man, "Which way should I go?" and once again the old man replied, "Go to your right." so once again the young man went to the left and once again the young man's choice caused him much peril, and once again the young man ultimately wound up right back where he had started at the same fork in the road but this time the old man was gone. As he stood there at the fork in the road trying to decide what to do, a young man tapped him on the shoulder and asked, "Which way do I go?"

It is just as hard for me to accept the fact that I am fifty-five years old, as it is for me to accept the role of the sage, mentor, or coach in this story. I certainly do not know what is best for you, but I do know what has worked for me, and that is what I have to give. I hope you laughed with me, cried with me, and were entertained by me, but most of all I hope that you learned something new from me, or at least thought about it in a new way and became willing to have a new experience with it. You may have entered your adult life better prepared with a full tool box full of quality sharpened tools to live by than I did or you may have been even more handicapped then I. Whatever the case, the primary theme of my journey is that if I can do it, anyone can do it, and if anyone can do it, that means *you* can do it. As for me, I know that where I am right now I am the best Bob I have ever been, and that is good enough for me today. Take what you like, and leave the rest!

Appendix

Recommended resources as they relate to each chapter's subject

Fear:
Carlos Castaneda, *The Fire from Within,* Pocket Books, 1984.
Susan Jeffers, *Feel the Fear and Do It Anyway,* Ballantine Books, 1987.
Susan Jeffers, *Feel the Fear and Beyond,* Random House, 1998.

Anxiety and Depression:
Helene Cho, *Hamster of the Wheel, Self-Published* 2010.

Reality:
Dalai Lama, *Be Here Now,* The Crown, 1971.
Eckhart Tolle, *A New Earth,* Plume, 2006.
Eckhart Tolle, *The Power of Now,* Namaste, 1999.

Relationships:
Gary Chapman, The Five Love Languages, Northfield, 2004.
David Deida, *Blue Truth, Sound True* 2005.
Harvile Hendrix, *Getting the Love You Want,* Owl Books, 1998.
Susan Jeffers, *Dare to Connect,* Ballantine Books, 1992.
Stephen and Alex Kendrick, *The Love Dare,* B&H Books, 2008.
Ernest Kurtz, *The Spirituality of Imperfect,* Bantam, 1992.
M. Scott Peck, *The Road Less Traveled,* Touchstone, 1978.
Tom Rath, *Vital Friends,* Gallup, 2006.
Don Miguel Ruiz, *The Four Agreements,* Amber-Allen, 1997.

Mechanics:
Duncan Mathison, *Unlock the Hidden Job Market,* FP Press, 2009.
Anthony Parinello, *Selling to VITO,* Adams, 1999.
Robin Ryan, *60 Seconds and You're Hired,* Penguin, 2000.
Robin Ryan, *Over 40 and You're Hired,* Penguin, 2009.

The Rest of the Story:
Dr. Wayne Dyer, *Living the Wisdom of the Tao,* Hay House, 2008.
Dr. Wayne Dyer, *Wishes Fulfilled,* Hay House, 2012.
—Dr. Dyer has written as least twenty-three other books that I know of, any one of which I would recommend. Furthermore, in each of his books he provides references to books that have inspired him.

CPSIA information can be obtained at www.ICGtesting.com
Printed in the USA
LVOW12s1435170813

348305LV00002B/2/P